LANCA．   ．．⌐

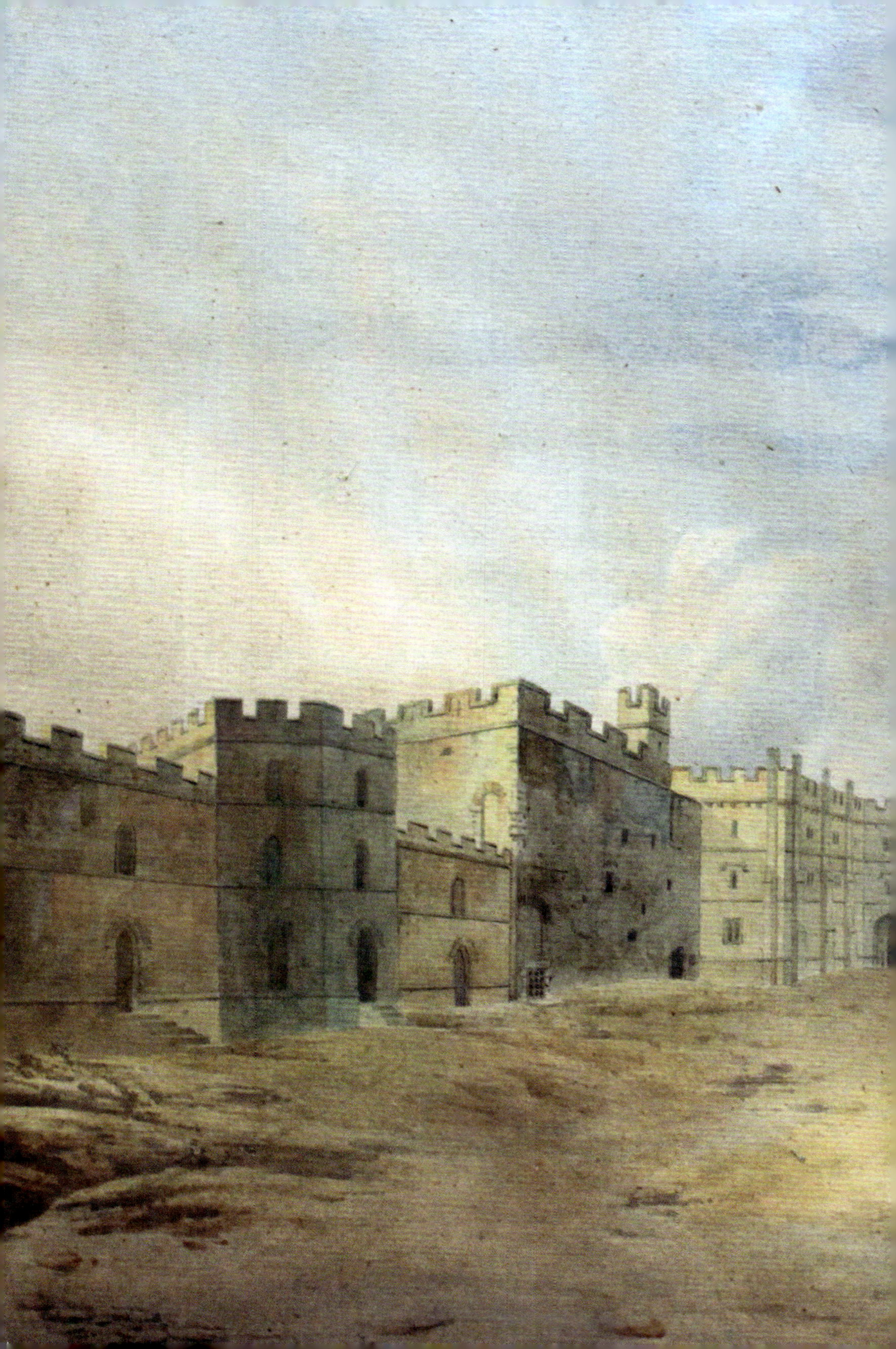

A HISTORY OF
LANCASTER CASTLE

COLIN PENNY AND GRAHAM KEMP

First published in 2022
by Palatine Books
Carnegie House
Chatsworth Road
Lancaster LA1 4SL
www.palatinebooks.com

Copyright © Colin Penny and Graham Kemp

All rights reserved
Unauthorised duplication contravenes existing laws

The right of Colin Penny and Graham Kemp
to be identified as the authors of this work has been asserted in
accordance with the Copyright, Designs and Patents act 1988

British Library Cataloguing-in-Publication data
A catalogue record for this book is available from the
British Library

Paperback ISBN 13: 978-1-910837-42-9

Designed and typeset by Carnegie Book Production
www.carnegiebookproduction.com

Printed and bound by Cambrian Printers

Front cover: Coat of Arms of the Duchy of Lancaster (reproduced by kind permission of the Duchy of Lancaster); photograph of main entrance © Carnegie Book Production
Back cover: Lancaster Castle *c.*1410 (Illustration by Terry Abbott); the tombstone of a cavalryman from the *Ala Augusta* (photograph by Colin Penny, used by kind permission of Lancaster City Museum); photograph of courtyard © Carnegie Book Production

Contents

Dedication	vi
Foreword	vii
Introduction	ix
The Romans on Castle Hill	1
Castle Foundation and Norman History, 1066–1260	12
Earldom and Dukedom of Lancaster	27
Lancaster Castle Assizes	44
Prisoners of Religious Conscience	57
The Lancashire Witches: 1612	71
The English Civil War and the Jacobites	83
Debtors	88
Notable Trials, Cases and Prisoners, 1795–1981	98
Prison Reform	116
Twentieth and Twenty-First Centuries	147
Further Reading	163

DEDICATION

This book is dedicated to all the tour guides at Lancaster Castle, past and present.

Danny Smith, guide and court keeper of the castle. Photo reproduced by kind permission of William Jefferies

Foreword

Lancaster Castle is one of the country's major historic monuments and for over 900 years has stood on the hilltop looking out over the river Lune and the city of Lancaster. Owned by Her Majesty the Queen in her role as Duke of Lancaster, the castle has a unique history and who better to tell that history than this book's joint authors Colin Penny and Graham Kemp. Between them they have almost 40 years of experience in managing the castle, researching its history and telling its tales to tourists from around the world.

As Constable of the Castle and keeper of the keys for Her Majesty the Queen, I am always impressed with their all-encompassing knowledge and am delighted that this first detailed history is now available for all to enjoy.

The authors recount the growth and development of the castle from medieval times to the present day, but also explore the use of the site during the Roman period. From its medieval keep to its impressive fifteenth-century gatehouse and splendid Georgian Shire Hall, the castle tells us much about the history of Britain and the county of Lancashire.

The authors describe its evolution from a military fortress to a prison and courthouse, prisoner of war camp, police training centre and major tourist attraction. Its history is still being unearthed and along with its tales of individual characters, notorious trials and barbaric hangings it tells much of Lancashire's economic and social history.

Much of the castle's history is as a centre of justice and part of it is still in use as a Crown Court. In fact, Lancaster Castle can boast one of the longest periods of unbroken use as a court building in the country.

Since ceasing to be used as a prison in 2011, the castle has undergone major repair, restoration and refurbishments by the Duchy of Lancaster. More and more has been opened up to the public. The old prison visitors' building has been demolished, revealing more of the original structures, including a beautiful, covered cloister walk. Lancaster University has a conference suite on site; Lancashire Constabulary has opened a museum in part of the old prison. The old prison workshops have been converted to provide offices, a boardroom and library for the Duchy of Lancaster, giving them a permanent presence in the castle and city. The courtyard is now a huge open space lending itself to a wide range of public events.

And so its history continues to evolve. As more people visit the castle and as more areas of the castle are opened for them to visit, this publication is timely and whets the appetite, both of those with minimal knowledge who may have yet to pay a visit and of those wanting a deeper insight and understanding.

Colin Penny and Graham Kemp give us an accurate historical account at the same time as bringing Lancaster Castle to life with their sometimes amusing and sometimes macabre anecdotes. This is no dry historical text, but a riveting story written by two people who, through working at the castle, have an intimate knowledge of the building and its history and are regularly unearthing new information and historical evidence.

Pamela Barker DL
Constable of Lancaster Castle

Introduction

This is not a guidebook to Lancaster Castle. Currently, access to most of the interior areas of the castle which can be visited by the public is by guided tour only, so to produce a guidebook would be superfluous to requirements. The guided tours are also amongst the best available at any site anywhere in the world, so to try and replicate the experience in a book would be a very tall order indeed. Rather, we believe this to be the first comprehensive history of Lancaster Castle to appear in a single volume dedicated solely to the topic. It is a history of Lancaster Castle from its earliest origins to the present day; it is designed to sit alongside the guided tour and offer a deeper insight into some areas of the castle's history than is possible in an hour. That said, neither is this an academic work; what we have aimed to produce is a readable and enjoyable canter through the castle's history, aimed at the general reader. This could be someone who has yet to visit the site or who, having had their appetite whetted by the tour, wishes to learn more about the building and some of the more prominent figures associated with it. This is the story of a royal fortress which lies at the heart of the Duchy of Lancaster. It also occupies an important and unrivalled position in the development of the city of Lancaster, in the history of Lancashire, and in the north of England in general. We hope you enjoy the experience.

Colin Penny and Graham Kemp
July 2022

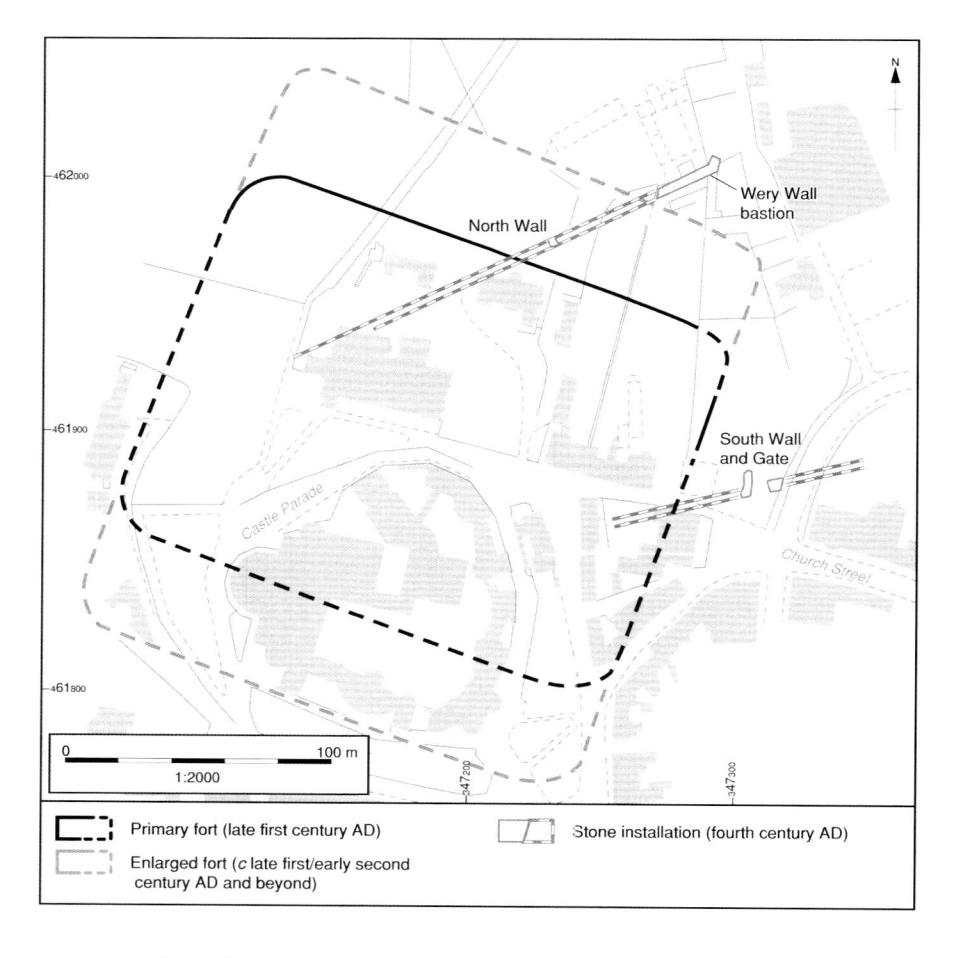

Plan of the early fort at Lancaster. Image reproduced courtesy of Oxford Archaeology Ltd

The Romans on Castle Hill

Although we know that Castle Hill has been occupied in one form or another for almost 2,000 years, comparatively little is known about those who lived and worked here prior to 1150. Very little archaeological investigation has been possible due to the working nature of Lancaster Castle as both a prison and a court building. The location of the Priory Church and its associated cemetery is another complication, so there are huge gaps in our knowledge. We do not know for sure if this site was occupied prior to the arrival of the Romans. Neither do we know what the Romans called Lancaster – Calunium is one possibility, Galacum another.

For many years it was believed that the first fort built in Lancaster by the Romans was constructed in about AD 79, which placed it during the governorship of Britain by Gnaeus Julius Agricola (AD 77–83). Agricola was the father-in-law of Rome's greatest historian, Cornelius Tacitus, who wrote a biography of him following his death in about AD 93. Understandably, Tacitus wanted to show Agricola in the best possible light, and in doing so he played down the achievements of Agricola's predecessors in Britain, particularly in the north west of England. This had a huge effect later, as archaeologists and historians tended to follow Tacitus, and credited Agricola with anything built in the region of roughly the right date. More recent analysis, however, has tended to revise these theories. It is now known, for example, that the forts at Carlisle, to the north of Lancaster, and that at Ribchester, to the south, predate Agricola's governorship. As a result, it is very likely that the first fort at Lancaster was built earlier than previously thought, in about

AD 74 when Petillius Cerialis was governor of Britain. He conducted a campaign in the north of England, against a tribe known as the Brigantes and, in the wake of this, ordered the construction of a number of garrison forts.

The function of the fort was to supervise and control the local population and it would have been the job of the soldiers stationed here to patrol, police and protect the surrounding area. The main gate faced eastwards and this suggests that the Roman commanders felt that any possible attack would come from this direction.

The ramparts were built from turf and timber, the fort being rectangular in shape (like a playing card) with guard towers at the corners and surrounded by a number of defensive ditches. All of the internal buildings, such as barracks, the commander's house, and the granaries would also have been constructed in timber. At over five acres in size, the fort was comparatively large and it is almost certain that cavalry were stationed here at this time. Archaeological evidence has been uncovered which proves the presence of two cavalry units, the *Ala Augusta* and the *Ala Sebosiana*, although the exact dates of when they were here is unknown. The spectacular tombstone of a cavalryman from the *Ala Augusta* was unearthed during construction work in the city and this can be seen in Lancaster City Museum. The accompanying dedication shows that the soldier came from Germany. A newspaper report from 1818 stated that when the medieval Dungeon Tower was being demolished to make way for the new Female Penitentiary, a large number of horses' teeth were found below the foundations [*Northern Star*, Number 14, July 1818]. Perhaps these were relics from that time.

At some point during the late first or early second centuries, the fort was enlarged considerably and re-orientated through 90 degrees so that it now faced north. The reason for the re-alignment must have been based on the belief that the main threat now came from tribes living in what is now southern Scotland. The Brigantes had been successfully conquered, but the Roman high command at that time was increasingly convinced that expansion into Scotland would not be feasible in the foreseeable future.

The tombstone of a cavalryman from the *Ala Augusta*. Photograph by Colin Penny. Used by kind permission of Lancaster City Museum

Therefore, the direction of possible attack was now much more likely to come from the north. Speculation continues as to why the fort was enlarged; one possibility is that two cavalry regiments were stationed here simultaneously. Another is that the fort had some additional, possibly administrative, function. Whatever the reason, the new fort may have occupied an area of up to nine acres.

The reconstruction of walls and internal structures in stone gave an added sense of permanence to the site.

The existence of a bathhouse in close proximity to the fort would also have been a necessity for the hygiene, entertainment and social life of the soldiers stationed at Lancaster. In order to generate the heat necessary to warm these buildings, bathhouses had their own furnaces which made them very susceptible to fire. As a result, they were invariably positioned outside the walls of the fort, but close enough to be accessible. Here soldiers and civilians alike would have enjoyed a sauna and bathing in hot pools to open up the pores. Their skin would then be scraped by attendants to remove the accumulated dirt and grime, before they plunged themselves into a cold bath to close the pores on their fresh clean skin. The whole experience took a considerable amount of time and friends would meet to while away the hours in conversation, gaming, eating and other pastimes. Today, it is possible to see the partial remains of a Roman bathhouse in a field just to the north of the castle, but it is believed that this particular one was not associated with the Roman fort. Rather, this was a private bathhouse attached to a large building, which has been variously interpreted as either a *mansio* (a kind of hotel for the needs of official

The bathhouse at Lancaster. Photograph by Colin Penny. Used by kind permission of Lancaster City Council

travellers), or the residence of an important local dignitary. The possibility of the latter being correct is bolstered by the discovery of an altar in 1797 whilst the foundations for the present Shire Hall were being dug. The altar bears a Latin inscription which translates as: *To the holy god Mars Cocidius, Lucius Vibinius Beneficarius Consularis, performs his vow willingly to a deserving object.*

Altar to Mars Cocidius at Lancaster Castle. Photograph by Colin Penny. Used by kind permission of Lancashire County Council Museum Service

Dating possibly to the second century, the dedication to Mars Cocidius represents the standard Roman practice of taking a British God (in this case the war god Cocidius) and assimilating it with the closest Roman counterpart (Mars). This policy of *Interpretatio Romana* ensured that local populations were able to continue to honour their traditional gods. At the same time, these gods were 'Romanised' by the addition of their Roman counterpart, thus helping to foster loyalty to Rome and the Roman gods.

The mention of the dedicator being a Beneficarius Consularis is interesting as this was a high-ranking official appointed by the governor of the province. What he was doing in Lancaster remains a mystery, but it has been speculated that he was connected in some way to the functioning of the port or to the taxation of goods arriving into it. His dedication to Cocidius is also interesting as references to this god tend to be found in the north east of England, suggesting that Lucius Vibinius had spent some time in that part of the country. Could he have been seconded from one of the garrisons along Hadrian's Wall, or at Newcastle, which was another important port during the Roman period?

There can be no doubt that the presence of a large number of soldiers with money to spend attracted considerable numbers of tradespeople and entrepreneurs to the area. In a comparatively short time, a civilian settlement (known as a *vicus*) grew up in close proximity to the fort. Soldiers represented a stable and well-paid market for a wide range of manufactured goods, foods and leisure services. Metalworkers, jewellers, leatherworkers, weavers, potters, bakers, inns and brothels were all to be found in the immediate vicinity. More luxurious goods could be imported through the developing port at Lancaster and sold to those who could afford them. Many soldiers also had families, despite the fact that until the reign of Septimius Severus (193–211) they were forbidden to marry while on active service. Their 'wives' and children could not be accommodated in the fort and so tended to live immediately outside in the *vicus*. On discharge (usually after 25 years of service), many soldiers would officially marry their loved ones of many years and legitimise their children, some of whom would go on to provide new recruits for their father's former unit.

Altar of Julius Januarius. Photograph by Colin Penny. Used by kind permission of Lancaster City Museum

Veterans were also allocated a plot of land on their discharge, the size of which was commensurate with their former rank. The Lancaster City Museum today houses an altar dedicated by Julius Januaris, a retired cavalryman, who resided in the area of modern-day Bolton-le-Sands.

In Lancaster, the modern streets of Church Street and Penny Street follow the lines of the major *viae* (streets) of the Roman civilian settlement; the former providing the main route to the east gate of the fort. It has been estimated that, by the second century,

View of modern-day Church Street from the site of the Roman fort's east gate. Photograph by Colin Penny

the population of the combined fort and settlement could have amounted to as many as 3,000 people.

It is probable that the fort was abandoned during the reign of Antoninus Pius (138–61), who moved the Roman frontier north from Hadrian's Wall to the Forth–Clyde line and established the Antonine Wall. Although this was itself abandoned, and the line of Hadrian's Wall re-established under his successor Marcus Aurelius (161–80), it seems that the fort at Lancaster may have remained unoccupied until the mid-third century. At this point, a smaller force was probably installed although little is known about it. This was a period of intense instability throughout the Roman Empire, with the effects of increased cross-frontier raiding and invasion exacerbated by internal rivalries and long-term civil war. The impact on society, the economy, agriculture and the military was devastating and, at times, it appeared that the empire, particularly in the west, would collapse. Some provinces broke away in an attempt to make it on their own, such as the so-called Gallic Empire (*Imperium Galliarum*), led by the rebel emperor Postumus, which included Gaul and Britain. Although ultimately unsuccessful, the effects of both the rebellion and subsequent reprisals were terrible, and the fact that the bath-house and basilica in Lancaster are recorded as being rebuilt in the 260s may be connected to these events. The rebellion was brought to an end in 273.

Continuing hostile incursion throughout the province of Britain during the fourth century, however, led to the construction of a number of coastal fortifications which have since become known as 'Saxon Shore' fortresses. These were much more like medieval castles than the previous forts, with thick towering stone walls and huge corner towers capable of accommodating Roman artillery, such as catapults, on their turrets. These were defensive structures and that at Lancaster was constructed in about 325. At this point the fort was again re-orientated, this time to face the west. Clearly it was now from the sea that attacks were expected to come and this is entirely in keeping with known raids by the Scotti (who occupied areas of modern-day Ireland). These new-style fortifications were huge and quite capable of housing not just those defending them, but also the civilian population of the adjacent *vicus* (in much the same way as medieval castles would do later). The seaward preoccupation of the defenders may be indicated by the garrisoning in the fort of a unit of bargemen (*numerus barcariorum*). It has been speculated that this irregular group of mariners may have patrolled the shallow waters of Morecambe Bay in order to reduce the possibility of a surprise attack on the exposed coastal area. The discovery of an inscribed stone altar (now on display at Lancaster Maritime Museum) provides firm evidence of the garrisoning of this unusual unit at Lancaster. Whether or not they were the only unit stationed in the fort remains unknown, but given their specialist role it seems unlikely. At this point, the garrison was

Altar of the *Numerus Barbariorum*. Photograph by Colin Penny. Used by kind permission of Lancaster Maritime Museum

probably mixed, with another unit providing the necessary land forces needed for a comprehensive defence of the area.

This fort probably continued in active use into the fifth century, although the exact date of its abandonment has not yet been determined. Indeed, following the departure of any organised Roman force, it was probably the case that the remains of the fort continued to provide protection and shelter for some considerable time. When the Normans arrived in the eleventh century, it is quite probable that large parts of the fort were still standing. Indeed, the surviving walls would have provided some sort of perimeter defence for any early Norman construction on the site. It is certain that the fort would have later provided a handy source of rubble for use in the construction of the walls and towers of the twelfth and also for additions made to the castle in the thirteenth century. Cut and dressed stone can be clearly seen in the exposed wall in-fill dating to the early thirteenth century.

Section of thirteenth-century wall in-fill showing the use of cut stone, probably from the Roman fort. Photograph by Colin Penny. Used by kind permission of Lancashire County Council Museum Service

Castle Foundation and Norman History, 1066–1260

I F YOU TRAVELLED TO THE NORTH WEST OF ENGLAND in 1066, the year of the Norman Conquest, you would find no county of Lancaster. Instead, the area was divided between three other counties. The land between the river Mersey and the river Ribble, known as *Inter Ripam et Mersam* (today's south Lancashire), was part of north Cheshire. The land north of the river Ribble, including the town of Preston, was in Yorkshire, while the small area around Lancaster was part of Northumberland. In the latter area you would have found, according to the Domesday Book, the manor of Halton – a royal manor belonging to the earls of Northumbria. The manor included two small villages, both carrying the name of Lancastre. The first, known simply as Lancastre, was a small hamlet on the site of the former Roman *vicus*. The other village was called Church Lancastre, and this lay on top of the hill where the Roman fort had once stood. It was probably centred on a Saxon predecessor of the current priory church, hence its name. Ten miles north from these villages lay the river Kent at Kendal and, if you had crossed the river there, you would have found yourself in Scotland.

Until 1018 the Lake District had been the last Welsh stronghold of northern Britain, called Cumberland – the Land of Cymri, but in 1018 this was absorbed into Scotland. In 1066 the King of Scotland, Malcolm III (1058–93), opposed the Norman takeover of England, and gave sanctuary to the last Saxon claimant, Edgar Atheling; he also married Edgar's sister, Margaret. Malcolm began a campaign to dispute the Norman possession of northern England, in particular the rich lands of Northumberland and Durham. Malcolm could threaten these lands from both Scotland and Cumberland, but in 1087 William the Conqueror's son, William II (known as William Rufus), began a military campaign to deal with this threat. By 1090, he had thrown the Scots out of Cumberland, pushing them back beyond Carlisle. It was this campaign that led to the foundation of Lancaster Castle in 1093.

One of William's most loyal supporters was a Norman baron named Count Roger de Poitou. His father, Roger de Montgomerie, the first Earl of Shrewsbury, had been William the Conqueror's trusted right-hand man. Roger's mother was Mabel de Bellême; the family came from southern Normandy, and they were typically ruthless for the period when pursuing their own interests. Mabel had taken to poisoning rivals to acquire their lands in Normandy, and in 1072 she had been beheaded in her own bed by a relative of one of her victims. Roger's older brother, Robert, who became the second Earl of Shrewsbury, was described by Oderic (1075–c.1142) as 'grasping and cruel, an implacable persecutor of the Church of God and the poor... unequalled in his iniquity in the whole Christian era'. His brutality is said to have inspired the legend of Robert Diablo – the Devil Baron.

In about 1068, Roger de Poitou had been given the lands of *Inter Ripam et Mersam*, and he established his castle at Penwortham, just south of Preston. This was a typical Norman wooden motte and bailey castle, which comprised an artificial mound (the motte), with a wooden tower (keep) upon it, surrounded by fenced courtyard (the bailey). His motte can still be seen in the churchyard at Penwortham. Following his support in the conquest of Cumberland, William Rufus rewarded Roger by allowing him to extend his lands north to the South Lakes. His lands would one day become most of modern Lancashire.

With his lands extended, Roger decided to move his castle from Penwortham to Church Lancastre, founding the castle there in 1093. The Normans brought castles to England to dominate their new lands. These were at first wooden structures which they literally brought with them on their ships to assemble on landing. Roger's castle at Lancaster would also have been assembled in

The Motte at Penworthham. Photograph by Jill Kemp. Reproduced by kind permission of St Mary's Church, Penwortham

this manner. However, the choice of Lancaster suggests that he was less concerned with dominating the region than defending it. Lancaster lies in a narrow gap between the Pennines to the east and the sea to the west, and any Scottish attack on his lands from the north would have had to pass through Lancaster. In addition, the river Lune blocks the gap, so the Scots would have had to cross at the main ford, which lay directly below the hill on which the castle was sited. That is the reason why Roger founded his castle in this location. In the following year he also established a Benedictine priory next to it for the salvation of his soul.

Although Roger's powerbase was centered in the north west with 300 manors, like all Norman barons, he had other manors scattered across England. These included 76 manors in Yorkshire, 59 in Suffolk, 44 in Lincolnshire, 11 in Nottinghamshire, 7 in Derbyshire, 10 in Norfolk, 3 in Essex and 1 in Suffolk. This was how the Normans distributed all the wealth they had gained from their

The former Benedictine priory next to the castle, established 1094, now Lancaster Priory Church

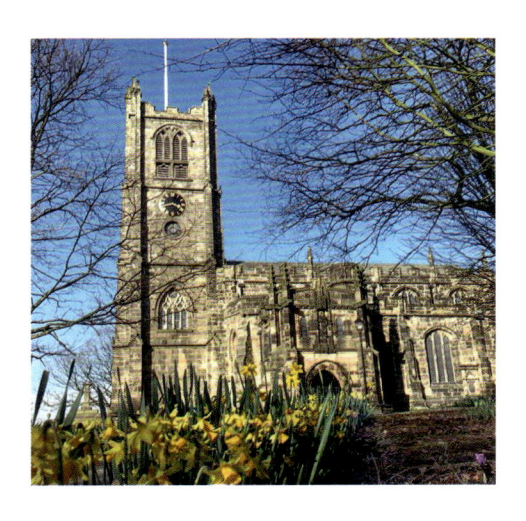

conquest of England amongst themselves. Such lands were given a collective title – they were known as an 'Honour'. Each honour was given a name to distinguish it from the others, often named after the Baron's chief base. So, Roger de Poitou's honour was known as the Honour of Lancaster, even though it included manors as far away as Boxted in Suffolk. The Honour would have little to do with the later formation of the County of Lancaster, but it would have everything to do with the creation of the future Earldom, and later Dukedom, of Lancaster.

On 2 August 1100, William Rufus was 'accidentally' killed whilst hunting in the New Forest. His younger brother, Henry, immediately seized the throne before his older brother, Robert, Duke of Normandy, could get back from Palestine, where he had been taking part in the First Crusade. When Robert returned, he was determined to pursue what he believed was his superior claim to the English throne. He invaded England with an army and met his brother Henry at Alton, in Hampshire. At the last minute, however, the two brothers met between their armies and Henry somehow persuaded his elder brother to return to Normandy. Later Henry invaded Normandy, captured his brother and imprisoned him in Cardiff Castle, where he wrote poetry until his death in 1134. Robert has a magnificent tomb which can be seen in Gloucester Cathedral.

During the struggle between Henry and Robert, Roger de Poitou and his brother Robert Belleme saw an opportunity to increase their own power by playing kingmaker. In 1102 they led a rebellion against Henry I (1100–35) in favour of Robert, but unfortunately for them it failed. The brothers were exiled and their lands and castles in England were confiscated. Many of Roger's manors in the *Inter Ripam et Mersam* were given to the Earl of Chester, whilst some of those north of the Ribble were given to the Taillebois family, who were the barons of Kendal. Henry I kept Lancaster Castle for himself, making it a royal castle, which it has remained ever since. The custodianship of the castle, however, was given over to the barons of Kendal which they retained for the next century. William, the fifth baron, even changed his name to 'de Lancaster', the first record of Lancaster being used as a surname. Roger de Poitou's brother-in-law, the Count of Mortain based in Normandy, also lost his title and land. This was given to Henry's favourite nephew, Stephen of Blois, along with Roger's Honour of Lancaster. For the next hundred years, the Honour would be part of the lands of the counts of Mortain. Stephen would later found Furness Abbey.

Henry I died in December 1135 and Stephen de Blois seized the throne in opposition to Henry I's named heir, his daughter Maud (1102–67). Maud found support in Henry I's oldest illegitimate son, Robert, Earl of Gloucester, and between them they challenged Stephen (1135–54) for the throne, plunging England into a 19-year civil war known as the 'Anarchy'. Taking advantage of this situation in 1138, King David I of Scotland (1124–53) invaded England in support of Maud and Robert. He took back Cumberland and demanded Northumberland. Stephen refused the latter, so the Scots struck deep into the north, plundering their way right down to Yorkshire. Interestingly, they did not invade or raid the north west. It was not worthy of their attention, being mainly a region of hills and marshes that was nowhere near as rich as the lands to the east. In the light of this perhaps Roger de Poitou need not have founded Lancaster Castle as a bastion against the Scots. There was a battle fought at Clitheroe (1138) where the Scots defeated the English. However, this was not a battle to defend the north west. The Scots (mainly from the borders and area of Glasgow) came down the Ribble valley to pre-empt an English attempt to attack them in Yorkshire via this route. Despite being heavily armoured, the English could not withstand the fierce charge of the Scots, and it was said the river Ribble ran with the blood of English knights. Once they had won the battle, the Scots retreated back into Yorkshire. There would not be another battle in the north west of England between Scots and the English until the Battle of Preston in 1648. Later that year Stephen defeated the Scots at the Battle of the Standard in North Yorkshire, but with Maud to the south and the Scots to the north, Stephen needed to prevent any future prospect of a Scottish invasion. He therefore gave all the lands north of the Tees in the east, and north of the Ribble in the west, to Scotland. Lancaster was now part of the Kingdom of Scotland, its castle a Scottish royal castle. It would remain so for the next 16 years

The war between Stephen and Maud continued until both sides were exhausted and it ended in a compromise. Stephen would be allowed to keep the throne, but it would be Maud's son Henry (not Stephen's son) who would succeed him as king. Stephen died soon afterwards. Henry II, shortly after becoming king in 1154, took back the lands given to Scotland; from 1157 Lancaster and its castle was once more in England. King Stephen's son, William, was compensated for the loss of the throne by being allowed to keep his father's title of the Count of Mortain, which included the Honour of Lancaster and the castle. On his death, it passed to his widow and, when she died in 1167, King Henry reclaimed it for himself. When Henry's son, Richard I, became king in 1189, he made his brother, Prince John, the Count of Mortain, leading to the long and important association of Prince John with the North West.

The Mystery of Lungess Tower

The Lungess Tower is the great stone keep at the centre of the castle. It stands 70 feet high, with each of the four sides 80 feet long, and 10 feet thick, and is the oldest part of the castle still standing. It was probably constructed in the twelfth century. This

The Keep. Photograph by Colin Penny. Used by kind permission of the Duchy of Lancaster

The Keep: East Elevation. Photograph by Colin Penny. Used by kind permission of the Duchy of Lancaster

Watercolour by Robert Freebairn showing the staircase to the first floor entrance of the keep prior to the construction of the Debtors' Wing. Reproduced by kind permission of Lancaster City Museum

was not uncommon, for at this time, the Normans were beginning to replace many of their wooden castles with stone structures. However, what is unusual about Lancaster's keep is the nature of the Lungess Tower. It is a spilt-keep design, with an internal spine wall running north–south, consisting of four great halls, and was built in a style similar to that of the Tower of London. The original entrance was not on the ground floor, but on the first floor along the southern wall. This entrance was built over when the Debtors' Wing was constructed between 1794 and 1796 and so is now no longer visible. In the event of an attack during which the enemy succeeded in getting inside the castle perimeter, the keep would act as a last line of defence. Having a narrow entrance, which could only be reached via a narrow flight of steps, meant that, at least in theory, it did not matter how many attackers there were as they could only enter the keep one at a time. As such, it was a very powerful and expensive structure. So why would an English king have wanted to build such a powerful keep at Lancaster?

After all, the Scots consistently attacked the North East, and several Scottish kings were captured or defeated invading Northumberland. They tended to avoid the north west because there was very little in the area to tempt them. If an English king was going to build such a powerful castle, surely it would have been in defence of richer Northumberland, not the poor marshy lands of Lancashire. In addition, despite the English kings keeping good records of their expenditure, no record has ever been found for the construction of the Lungess Tower. However, for 16 years Lancaster was a part of Scotland, and whilst the kings of Scotland may not have been interested in invading the poor lands south of Lancaster, they were interested in keeping the mineral rich lands of Cumberland to the north, which they had previously lost to England in 1090.

King David I of Scotland was so delighted to regain Cumberland that he gave his son Henry the title 'Prince of Cumberland'. It follows, therefore, that David of Scotland would have gone to the expense of building such a strong and impressive keep. Hence, a castle originally founded by Roger de Poitou to defend the north west from Scottish attack, was now rebuilt to defend Scottish-acquired lands from English invasion. We may even add that the kings of Scotland were not so good at keeping records, which may explain the lack of any account for its construction. If David did build the Lungess Tower, then it would be possible to date it to the mid-1140s, allowing Lancaster to claim to be the most southern royal castle ever built by the Scots. For now we can only speculate, but perhaps in the future some record of its construction will be found and the mystery finally solved. Whoever built the Lungess Tower, they turned a small wooden ex-baronial castle in a remote region of England into a powerful royal fortress that could not be ignored. The building of the Lungess Tower put Lancaster Castle firmly on the map, leading to the founding of the town of Lancaster and the County of Lancaster in the decades following its construction.

With the death of David I (1153), the Scots could not hold on to their English possessions which were lost soon afterwards.

King John and Lancaster Castle 1189–1215

Following Henry II's death, in 1189, Prince John fought a short war with his brother, King Richard I (1189-99). It was during this conflict that Lancaster Castle sustained its first known attack when a force led by Theobald Walter (the brother of the Archbishop of Canterbury, Hubert Walter) came to take the castle in 1194. The

Lancaster Town Charter. Reproduced by kind permission of Lancaster City Council

The present fifteenth-century gatehouse. A portion of King John's earlier gatehouse can be seen on the far left. Photograph by Colin Penny. Used by kind permission of the Duchy of Lancaster

Interior of Hadrian's Tower. Photograph by Colin Penny. Used by kind permission of Lancashire County Council Museum Service

Interior of Hadrian's Tower. Photograph by Colin Penny. Used by kind permission of Lancashire County Council Museum Service

Present-day upper floor of Hadrian's Tower. The gallery is a Georgian addition of the late eighteenth century. Photograph by Colin Penny. Used by kind permission of Lancashire County Council Museum Service

castle surrendered without a fight, and Theobald was created sheriff of the county as a reward.

Despite this setback, it seems that Prince John had a continued affection for what was one of the first of his royal castles, and paid special attention to it. In 1193 he awarded the small village of Lancaster a town charter, so that there would be a town next to his royal castle. He then spent money on developing the castle's defences and, following his ascension to the throne in 1199, he decided to visit it. This was momentous occasion. He did not come immediately, as he spent money on improving the accommodation in preparation for the visit, but in 1206 he arrived and stayed on the second floor of the keep. It is said he took a liking to the region, one of the few English kings to do so.

Following his visit he decided to spend the modern equivalent of approximately £500,000 on further development, which formed the second-largest building programme of his reign. It would employ 30 masons, 83 labourers, 3 smiths and carpenters, and take over three years to complete. A new twin-tower gatehouse was built, and one tower of that gatehouse can still be seen as part of the present fifteenth-century gatehouse. Two new round towers were also constructed, and one of these has survived to the present day – Hadrian's Tower. At this time round towers were the latest development in military architecture, having been first encountered by European armies during the Crusades. These structures could withstand undermining far more successfully than square towers and provided overlapping fields of fire against attacking armies. Hadrian's Tower also contained a fighting gallery – a narrow passage into which any defenders could retreat as a last line of defence should the castle be attacked and the enemy succeed in getting inside the tower. In addition, John had a moat (ditch) constructed around the south side of the castle, but the steepness of the east and north sides made a ditch too difficult to dig and, in any case, superfluous. In the 1790s much of the moat was filled in to build the new Shire Hall. Part of the moat to the south of the castle survived until 1850 when the Board of Health ordered it to be filled in for health reasons.

King John also constructed the 'Crown Building' at the rear of the castle. Its lower floor was probably a stable block (now

Lancaster Castle c.1410. Illustration by Terry Abbott

the Old Cells), but the upper room was to be the site of the new criminal Assizes court for the County of Lancaster. John's father, Henry II (1154–89), had created the system of Assizes in 1166 as he wanted to establish his justice firmly throughout the kingdom. Henry initially used his country-wide network of royal castles to hold his courts, and Lancaster, now a substantial royal castle, would have been used for such. However, it would be John who would establish that the Lancashire Assizes were permanently held at the castle, building a Crown Court for the County Assizes. To this day Lancaster Castle still hosts a working Crown Court, making it England's oldest working castle, having administered the monarch's justice continuously for over 800 years. With the Assizes came a need to hold the prisoners awaiting trial and so Lancaster Castle also became a working prison. In addition to the Assizes,

Lancaster gained the sole right to host all of the county's public executions, which gave the new town of Lancaster a tourist trade.

Finally, King John is known to have commissioned work on what is referred to as the 'King's Lodgings'. The exact location of this building is unknown, but it is unlikely to have been either one of the round towers. It is known, however, that a large medieval arch on the first floor of Hadrian's Tower led into another gable-ended building, which was demolished just prior to the construction of the debtors' prison in 1794. Given that Hadrian's Tower is known to have contained an oven (the tower was sometimes referred to as 'John O'Gaunt's Oven'), it is possible that the King's Lodgings abutted Hadrian's Tower and that food was prepared in the latter before being taken through a connecting door to be served to any dignitaries lodging at the castle.

For many, John is regarded as a 'bad' king, but he was one of the best for the north west, and it was possibly due to him that our part of the country became the shire county of Lancaster. This was likely named after the castle, rather than the small newly created town of Lancaster. Lancashire would be the last shire county to be created in England. John also founded the town of Liverpool and he

Thirteenth-century entrance to the King's Lodgings from Hadrian's Tower? Photograph by Colin Penny. Used by kind permission of Lancashire County Council Museum Service

brought order and importance to what had been regarded by many kings since the tenth century as a lawless wild region of England. No other monarch would pay so much attention to the region until the reign of Queen Elizabeth II. For the next century and a half, the sheriffs of the county would be drawn from some of the most powerful men in the land. Ultimately, however, Lancashire would regress to being a backwater of the kingdom – an area of little importance until the Industrial Revolution.

When John died, in 1216, the Honour of Lancaster passed to his nine-year-old son, Henry III (1216–72) The Count of Mortain's lands and title had disappeared when John lost Normandy in 1204; the custody of Lancaster Castle was given over to Ralph de Blundeville, the sixth Earl of Chester. Ralph was the last great Earl of Chester, and, when he died childless in 1232, his estates were divided between his sisters. His sister Alice gained the earl's manors between the Ribble and the Mersey, which now came into the possession of her husband William de Ferrers, the fourth Earl of Derby. This passed, in 1247, to his son William, the fifth Earl of Derby, and then, in 1260, to Robert de Ferrers, the sixth earl. Between 1243 and 1254 Henry III spent over £380 on Lancaster Castle, which included works to the keep and gatehouse. The earlier accounts also mention work to the palisade, but the later ones mention work on the walls, and this might suggest that the last portions of wooden palisade were replaced with stone walls in 1254. Subsequently, the Honour of Lancaster, and the castle with it, was granted to Henry III's brother-in-law, Simon de Montfort, Earl of Leicester. The subsequent actions of both Robert de Ferrers and Simon de Montfort would bring about the creation of the Earldom, and later the Dukedom, of Lancaster.

Earldom and Dukedom of Lancaster

In the 1260s Simon de Montfort (c.1205–65) led a rebellion against King Henry III for the control of the government of the country. Simon came from an illustrious French military family, but he had few prospects in France. However, he had acquired the right to the Earldom of Leicester, but without the lands attached as these had been confiscated from Simon's father by King John. In 1230, Simon came to England to claim the title and lands, which he formally achieved in 1239 following a grant from the Earl of Chester who had acquired them. A year earlier Simon had married King Henry III's sister, Eleanor, and his lands, power and prestige were significantly increased. As a result of the marriage he gained control of a vast amount of land, including the rich wool county of Leicester – the wealthiest of England's medieval counties. Whilst he took the title Earl of Leicester, his lands also included the Honour of Lancaster. Following a rebellion against the king, in 1264, Simon reached the height of his power when he defeated and captured Henry III at the Battle of Lewes. To shore up his support in the country he looked beyond the barons, and courted the lesser nobility, the knights, and the emerging mercantile class – the town burgesses. The parliament he convened in 1265, therefore, was the first to include the 'commons' and began the process which would eventually lead to the establishment of a House of Commons in order to bring these knights and burgesses into the governance of England. Each county would send two shire knights and each borough two burgesses. This parliament was held on 20 January

1265, but later that year Simon de Montfort's rebellion was crushed and he was killed at the Battle of Evesham. The first record of the county of Lancaster sending representatives to a parliament occurs 30 years later when two attended the session in 1295.

Following Simon's death, Henry III regained control of the kingdom, and he awarded de Montfort's lands and the title Earl of Leicester to this second son Edmund Crouchback (1245–96). 'Crouch' is an Old English world for cross, and Edmund was a former crusader. As Edmund's new lands also included the Honour of Lancaster, in 1267, Edmund was given the new title, Earl of Lancaster. The two earldoms and their lands eventually became one, and the Earldom of Lancaster became one of the richest and most powerful earldoms in England. To this earldom was added the manor of Savoy in London, which was bestowed on Edmund by his mother, Eleanor of Provence, and named after her uncle Peter of Savoy. Thereafter, the Savoy Palace would become the earl's base in the capital. In 1381 the palace was destroyed during the Peasants' Revolt, but the manor (now the Strand) remains part of the Duchy of Lancaster to the present day and the offices of the Duchy are on the Strand.

The tomb of Edmund Crouchback (1245–96), who became Earl of Leicester in 1267, at Westminster Abbey. He was also the first Earl of Lancaster. Copyright: Dean and Chapter of Westminster

For his part in supporting Simon's rebellion, Robert de Ferrers had his lands confiscated and they were also added to the Earldom of Lancaster. To this day, the de Ferrers' home at Tutbury Castle remains part of the Duchy estate. In addition, Robert de Ferrers' rights over the lands between the Mersey and the Ribble were also added to the Earldom of Lancaster. This meant that the earldom now had rights over the whole of the county, and that would later prove greatly significant for Lancashire. The earldom was by this point one of the wealthiest ever created, boasting towns and manors in every county of England. It also held manors in Wales (Ogmore), and France (Beaufort in Champagne). The region of Beaufort had come to the earldom via Edmund's second wife, Blanche of Artois, Countess of Champagne, who was the niece of the king of France. The main town of her lands was Provins in Champagne, known throughout medieval Europe for growing a particular flower that was turned into condiments, toilet water and sweets. This was the Red Rose, the Rosa Gallica. Edmund adopted this rose as the symbol of his earldom, and many people believe this to be the origin of the red rose of Lancaster. Later, when the second Duke of Lancaster, John O'Gaunt (1340–99), wanted to give his illegitimate children a surname he called them 'Beaufort' after his French manor.

Edmund was determined to use the earldom to establish a junior branch of the royal family. In this he could use the royal coat of arms, the three leopards, but

The ornate plasterwork of the Shire Hall, showing the Rosa Gallica, the symbol of Edmund's earldom, and perhaps the origin of the Red Rose of Lancashire. Photograph by Carnegie Publishing. Used by kind permission of Lancashire County Council Museum Service

it had to have cadency on in it (a pattern) to show he was not of the main family. The type of cadency he used was a label, and to avoid confusion (as a blank label symbolises the eldest son of the monarch) Edmund used a pattern on the label to indicate it represented the junior branch. For this he chose a feature of his wife's coat of arms – the gold fleur-de-lys on a blue background. This was the first time an English coat of arms ever incorporated the French coat of arms and it has remained that of the Duchy of Lancaster ever since. The Earls of Lancaster based themselves at either the Savoy Palace or Leicester Castle, but never at Lancaster.

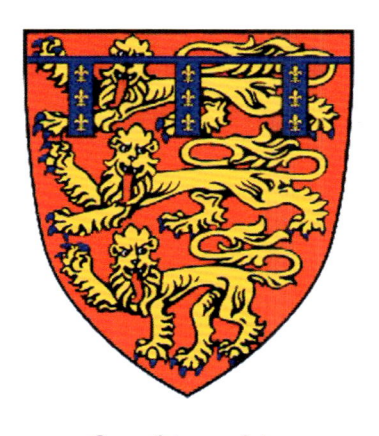

Coat of Arms of the Duchy of Lancaster. Reproduced by kind permission of the Duchy of Lancaster

The second earl, Thomas of Lancaster (c.1278–1322), rebelled against his cousin, King Edward II (1307–27), but his failure and execution led to the dissolution of the earldom in 1322. Thomas' younger brother Henry persuaded the next king, Edward III, to restore it and he became the third earl in 1327. Henry died at Leicester Hospital in 1345, and due to the care he was shown, left a legacy to the hospital which is still honoured by the Duchy to this day.

In the same year as Thomas, Earl of Lancaster, was killed (1322), Robert the Bruce (king of Scotland 1306–29) ravaged the north west of England as far south as Preston. Known as the Great Raid, he met very little resistance and inflicted considerable damage throughout the region, including to both the castle and town of Lancaster. It was probably in response to this that the Well Tower was constructed. Analysis on some of the internal timbers using dendrochronology has suggested that it was built in about 1330, and this would fit in well with a decision to strengthen the castle's defences in the wake of Bruce's attack. Clearly, the improvements carried out under King John had proved insufficient to withstand the Scottish raid, and it is significant that the area chosen for this tower faced the town. John's two towers had faced Morecambe Bay, and this was undoubtedly the direction from which the Scots approached in 1322. However, it may have been the case that they were then able to swing around the castle and attack the more lightly defended eastern section of wall, as here it may have remained only a timber palisade. If that were the case, it would be reasonable to suppose, that alongside the construction of the Well Tower, the sections of wall adjoining it were also rebuilt in stone. The Well Tower is a two-storey structure, which would have projected out from the wall in order to allow the maximum amount of firepower to be brought upon any attack from the arrow slits on all three projecting sides. The tower contained one of the castle's wells, hence its name, which still contains water to this day. Finally, there was an underground vaulted 'dungeon', or storeroom, and tradition has it that it was in this space that the Lancashire witches were imprisoned prior to their trial in 1612.

The Well Tower: Rear Elevation. Photograph by Colin Penny. Used by kind permission of the Duchy of Lancaster

Another tower possibly built at this time was the Dungeon Tower, which was demolished in 1818 to make way for the Female Penitentiary. The tower is recorded in a number of watercolours undertaken by Robert Freebairn in the 1790s. What can be seen is that it was clearly medieval in date, although somewhat larger than the Well Tower. Its position, between Hadrian's Tower and the gatehouse, can be seen as plugging a gap in the southern defences similar to that of the Well Tower in the east. It would be likely that the curtain wall connecting it to the gatehouse was also rebuilt in stone at the same time. The fact that it had become known as the Dungeon Tower by the Georgian period leaves no doubt as to its

The Dungeon Tower (on the left) as recorded by Robert Freebairn in his watercolour of the 1790s. Reproduced by kind permission of Lancaster City Museum

function by that time, but its original purpose would have been military. Interestingly, two other medieval towers are shown on the earliest-known depiction of Lancaster Castle which was created as part of a survey of the site in 1562. They can be seen on the right of

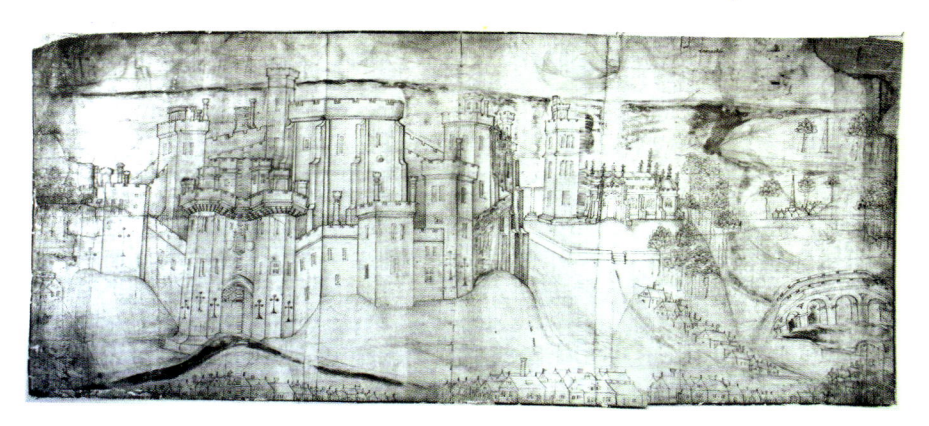

The earliest-known depiction of Lancaster Castle, created as part of a survey of the site in 1562. Reproduced by kind permission of Lancaster City Museum

the plan, behind what is clearly the Well Tower. These were demolished when the castle was demilitarised following the English Civil War and their date cannot be known. However, as the wall of c.1330 seems to pass in front of one of them, this suggests that at least one of these towers was earlier than the fourteenth century and enclosed by the later work.

The Duchy of Lancaster 1351–2017

If there was ever a King Arthur personified it was Edward III (1327–77), who led his knights in shining armour in victorious campaigns against the French, with more than a little help from the English peasant archers. He adopted the warlike St George as the patron saint of England, rather than the widely venerated, but rather more peaceful, St Edward the Confessor, and established a chivalric knightly order – the Order of the Garter, which was his equivalent of the Round Table. The first to join this new brotherhood was Edward's most loyal friend, outstanding diplomat, and foremost general, Henry de Grosmont (c. 1310–61), the fourth Earl of Lancaster.

In 1337 Edward had made his son, Edward the Black Prince (1130–76), the Earl of Cornwall, but he did not want his son to be on the same level as other earls. So, he used the continental term *Duce* or *Dux* to create a new level above an earl. Hence, the Dukedom of Cornwall is the oldest dukedom in England. In 1351 Edward rewarded his great friend Henry de Grosmont by also raising his status to that of a duke. Thus, the Duke of Lancaster is the second oldest dukedom, but initially it was only given for the lifetime of Henry himself. Henry had two daughters, Maud of Leicester and Blanche of Lancaster. Maud died childless, so Blanche inherited the whole of her father's estate in 1362, making her one of the richest heiresses in England – it is estimated that she was worth £43 billion in modern money. She was also one of the great beauties of Edward III's court, in both looks and manner, and was described as such by the great contemporary writer, Geoffrey Chaucer. Blanche (1342–68) was an independently minded girl with an indulgent

John O'Gaunt by Claude Nimmo. Reproduced by kind permission of the Duchy of Lancaster

father. Unusually for such a rich heiress, she was not betrothed by her mid-teens. This was the time of chivalry, and nobles were brought up on the stories of King Arthur, quests, and romantic love; Blanche wanted this kind of experience, and she was not to be disappointed. She was wooed by a tall, clever, handsome 17-year-old with a dark complexion. To the delight of her father, the 17-year-old was none other than the king's third son, John O'Gaunt (Ghent), and the relationship would develop into one of those rare love matches among noble houses. They married on 19 May 1359 at Reading Abbey, but Blanche died of plague at a tragically young age at Tutbury Castle, to the heartbreaking distress of John.

In 1361 Henry, the first Duke of Lancaster, died and with his death the title was extinguished. John O'Gaunt was made the fifth Earl of Lancaster, but one year later Edward III restored the dukedom and so John became the second Duke of Lancaster. In 1377, Edward III even added the gift of the county of Lancaster for John to rule as his own fiefdom. But how could the king give a county of England to another person to rule? The answer is that he did not; counties were (and still are) only an administrative district. For John O'Gaunt to 'rule' the county of Lancashire it had to be promoted to the status of a 'county palatine'. A palatinate in England was a legal construct which allowed a portion of the country to be given to a nobleman to rule on the monarch's behalf. It gave the recipient rights over justice and feudal dues from the crown tenants within that palatinate. Edward had already made the county of Lancaster a county palatine for the first duke in 1351, but only for his lifetime. While Edward restored the dukedom for his son in 1363, Lancaster only became a county palatine again with John as its ruler in 1377. It is likely that John O'Gaunt only visited Lancaster Castle twice – in 1385 and 1393. Edward III died in 1377, and was succeeded by his grandson Richard of Bordeaux, who became King Richard II (1377–99). He was also John O'Gaunt's nephew, and this monarch extended the 'rule' of the county palatine to all of John's heirs. Henceforth, Lancashire remains to the present day a county palatine with the Dukes of Lancaster still holding sovereign rights within it.

Unfortunately for the Duke of Lancaster, Richard II was avaricious and a great spendthrift, so he set his eyes on the wealth of the Dukedom of Lancaster. He dared not act against his uncle 'Old John of Gaunt, time honoured Lancaster', as Shakespeare would later call him, so he acted against John's heir, Henry Bolingbroke. In 1398, Richard had Henry banished from England for ten years on a spurious charge of conspiracy and on 5 February 1399, two days after John O'Gaunt's death, he declared Henry's banishment permanent and seized the dukedom. However, Henry returned to England later in the year to reclaim his inheritance and captured the

Tomb of Henry IV and Joan of Navarre, at Canterbury Cathedral.
Copyright: Canterbury Cathedral Archives and Library

king. Not only did he reclaim the dukedom, but he took the throne as well and was crowned Henry IV on 13 October 1399. Richard either died a natural death or was murdered whilst a prisoner in Pontefract Castle. Henry IV was concerned that his heirs may lose the crown and so protected the dukedom for them by insisting it remain a separate inheritance for his male heirs.

It was during the reign of Henry IV (1399–1413) that Lancaster Castle acquired a new and magnificent barbican gatehouse. Although known as the John O'Gaunt Gatehouse, this is a misnomer as it was certainly not built by him. This is proven by one of the two shields positioned on either side of the statue of John O' Gaunt. This shows the royal coat of arms comprising the three leopards of England, quartered with the three fleur-de-lys of the French monarchy (by this time the monarchs of England also claimed to rule France). Prior to 1403, the French coat of arms had contained more than three fleur-de-lys and, following the change of the French royal arms, Henry IV also changed his coat of arms. As a result, the gatehouse cannot be the work of John O'Gaunt who died in 1399, four years before the change took place. The other coat of arms is that of Henry's son and heir, Prince Henry (later Henry V), who was Duke of Lancaster at the time. The Pipe Rolls of both Henry IV and Henry V (1413–22) show that both of these kings devoted considerable sums of money to the upkeep of the

The Gatehouse. Photograph by Colin Penny. Used by kind permission of the Duchy of Lancaster

The coats of arms of Henry IV and his son Henry, Prince of Wales, either side of John O'Gaunt's statue. Photograph by Colin Penny. Used by kind permission of the Duchy of Lancaster

castle. Regarding the statue of John O'Gaunt, this was sculpted by Claude Nimmo, and was not added to the gatehouse until 1822.

As with the construction of the Well Tower and Dungeon Tower, this new building project followed a major attack on the town and castle by the Scots in 1389. The gatehouse stands 65 feet high, comprising of two massive octagonal towers equipped with arrow slits with overlapping fields of fire and 'murder holes', positioned high up, through which boiling liquid could be poured down onto hostile forces who might be attacking the main gate.

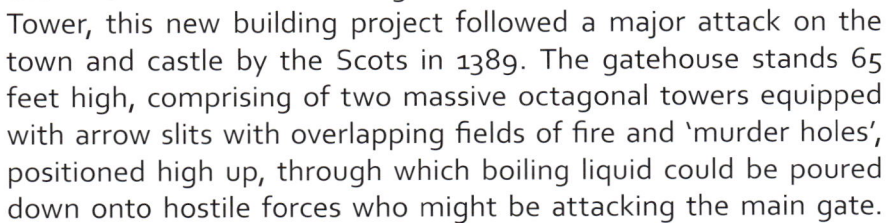

Inside, it contained six large rooms (three on each floor), and the names of some of these rooms survived down to the nineteenth century when they were used as debtors' accommodation. They allow us an insight into their original use, with names such as 'The Constables' and 'The Chancery'. The earlier gatehouse, which was built by King John, was not demolished to make way for the new building. Rather, it was

Artist's impression of the Chancery. Engraving by Thomas Physick, after drawing by Edward Slack. Reproduced by kind permission of Lancashire County Council Museum Service

incorporated within the new one. Traces of one of the earlier towers can be seen at the rear of the John O'Gaunt Gatehouse, as can the original archway at the front, behind the now static portcullis. The equipment used to raise and lower the portcullis remains in situ on an upper floor of the gatehouse.

In 1461, during the Wars of the Roses, Edward, Duke of York, took the throne from Henry IV's grandson, King Henry VI (1422–61 and 1470–71). Crowned King Edward IV (1461–83), he was faced with a dilemma with regard to the Dukedom of Lancaster. Technically, although Edward held the title and lands by right of conquest, he was unable to 'claim' them because he was not a descendant of the House of Lancaster. However, he knew them to be too powerful and wealthy to be in anyone else's hands, so he established that all the lands of the dukedom be incorporated into an entity which he termed the 'Duchy of Lancaster'. This was to be held 'forever to us and our heirs, Kings of England,' but he added the clause 'separate from all other possessions'.

In 1476, Edward IV planned to visit Lancaster on a progress of his northern lands. The county palatine had gained a reputation for outstanding lawless during the wars, and armed bands violently roamed the land. In 1454 rioters had even tried to storm the castle, causing £75 to be spent on its defence. In 1480 the Mayor of Lancaster wrote that the elections of that year had to be abandoned due to violent intimidation from those

Details of the gatehouse showing the original thirteenth-century arch behind the portcullis. Photograph by Colin Penny. Used by kind permission of the Duchy of Lancaster

without the town. Law and order were breaking down, and Duchy tenants were not paying their dues. One purpose of the 1476 progress was to re-establish royal and Duchy authority.

In October 1476, a letter was sent to the keepers of the parks of Quernmore and Radholme to supply timber for repairs at Lancaster Castle under the guidance of Lord Stanley, to a total cost of £155. In a report

The equipment used to raise and lower the portcullis, in-situ on an upper floor of the gatehouse. Photograph by Graham Kemp. Used by kind permission of the Duchy of Lancaster

detailing the repairs needed to the castle we have the earliest full description of the medieval buildings. The report stated that the keep was in need of repair due to the floor beams having become 'feeble'; it also mentions weeds and elder growing out of its walls. The keep was described as having three floors, with two great halls on each of the first and second floors, whilst the ground floor was used as the castle stables. Next to the keep was the medieval court building, which today houses the Court Library and the Old Cells. The walls were described as covered in shingles and in need of repair. The report also mentioned that a bay in the middle of the court building had fallen down. There was also a reference to a 'Jury House' lying west of the court building; this was presumably of wooden construction as it was stated that it would have to be rebuilt with Stanley's timber due to its poor condition at the time. The newly built gatehouse was described as in good condition, except for some damage to a 'southern high chamber' caused by a fallen chimney. It also referred to the castle as having three towers. One was called the 'Prison House', which can probably be identified with the Dungeon Tower. Again, it required attention to the floors which were described as being in a poor state. A 'Receiver's Tower' was also mentioned, which was said to be in a good state, and this was almost certainly the Well (or Witches') Tower. The final tower was described as 'begonne of old tyme', and stood not more than ten feet above the ground. The report also called for the north wall down to the Receiver's Tower to be embattled like rest of the castle walls. The north wall and tower lay across the middle of what is now the lower courtyard, on a line between the Well Tower and the north east corner of the keep.

In 1485, the first Tudor monarch, Henry VII (1485–1509), had parliament confirm the entities of the dukedom and Duchy. Henry VII added that it was to be managed separately from the crown for the benefit of all future kings of England. A committee, the Duchy Council, was established to manage the estates and manors for the monarch. This committee was headed by the Chancellor of the Duchy, who also oversaw the rule of the Palatinate of Lancaster, for example, in the appointment of the magistrates and the high sheriffs.

Since 1974, the Duchy has also been responsible for appointing the sheriffs of the new metropolitan counties of Merseyside and Greater Manchester, who, while no longer in the county, are still part of the Palatinate of Lancaster. In the appointment of a high sheriff it was traditional that, if there were more than one nomination, the monarch selected the sheriff by the use of a pin (a bodkin) – a

A cast of the commemorative inscription incorporated into the northern face of the keep at the time of its restoration, which reads 'ER' (Elizabeth Regina) 'RA' (Ralph Asshetor) 1585. Photograph by Colin Penny. Used by kind permission of Lancashire County Council Museum Service

The Duchy of Lancaster Bodkin, used for appointing the high sheriffs of the Palatinate of Lancaster Reproduced by kind permission of the Duchy of Lancaster

practice dating back to Elizabeth I (1558–1603). In the appointment of the Duchy sheriffs, a special Duchy pin is used and is housed at Lancaster House on the Strand.

The Tudor monarchs regarded the Duchy as of great significance and appointed their best minsters, such as Thomas More, Robert Cecil and Francis Walsingham, to run it for them. Elizabeth I declared the whole Duchy as 'one of the most famous, princeliest and stateliest pieces of the Queen's inheritance'. A survey of the Duchy castles in the north of England was commissioned in 1562 and a plan of Lancaster Castle was produced. In 1578, £235 was spent on repairs to the keep, and in 1585, the keep, Well Tower, and probably the Dungeon Tower, were all increased in height. The latter work was commissioned in the light of rising political tensions between England and Spain and an increasing fear of invasion. The order for the restoration stated that the castle shall 'be mayntayned and kepte, because it is a great strength to the countrie, and succour to the Queen's Justices'. A number of other castles around the English coast were also strengthened at this time. At Lancaster, a commemorative inscription was incorporated into the northern face of the keep, which reads 'ER' (for Elizabeth Regina) 'RA' (for Ralph Assheton, the high sheriff at the time) 1585.

For the Stuart monarchs who succeeded Elizabeth, however, the Duchy was regarded as simply a source of money independent from parliament to pay for their court life and their wars. Therefore, by the time of Queen Anne (1702–14), the Duchy was a shadow of its former self, having been heavily mortgaged and much of its lands alienated. By 1760, the Duchy had reached its lowest ebb with profits of just over £16 per annum.

In 1760, George III (1760–1820), who was deeply in debt and unable to pay for his government, surrendered the crown estates to parliament in exchange for the annual 'Civil List' payment, in effect receiving a salary. Such was the low value of the Duchy at the time that it was overlooked in the deal. Some have suggested that its low valuation may have been a deliberate ploy, as the Duchy's value suddenly began to rise almost immediately afterwards. The king appointed Lord Strange as its new Chancellor, and he began to reorganise the Duchy lands, improving efficiency and revolutionising the farming methods of its estates. By 1838 it was turning a profit of £5000. Parliament now applied to have the Duchy brought under its control but Queen Victoria (1837–1901) blocked the move. In 1896 its profit had risen to £60,000 and, by 2017, the profit was £18 million. The importance of the Duchy to the monarch can be seen by the fact that the Chancellor of the Duchy of Lancaster is not only a government post, but a cabinet one; the only royal Duchy to have this honour. In recent years, prominent politicians, such as Norman Tebbit, Kenneth Clarke, Mo Mowlem and Ed Milliband, have all been Duchy chancellors.

The Duchy today is not as great a landowner as it once was, but it still has estates in Wales, Cheshire, Lincolnshire, Leicestershire, Lancashire (including the foreshore of the county palatine) and Staffordshire. The majority of the Duchy lands are in Yorkshire, with the estates at Pontefract, Pickering, Goatshead and Knaresborough amounting to over 16,000 acres. Its most valuable real estate is the Strand in London, where its office is based at Lancaster House. A recent clerk of the Duchy proclaimed though that, whilst the head of the Duchy is at the Strand, its heart is always in the castle that gave the Duchy its name.

After Henry IV, few Dukes of Lancaster ever visited Lancaster Castle and none visited at all between 1618 and 1851. In celebration of the founding of the Duchy, Queen Victoria paid a brief visit in 1851 and, from then on, each Duke has paid at least one visit to the castle, with the

The special throne, carved by Gillows of Lancaster for Queen Victoria, now kept in the Grand Jury Room. Photograph by Carnegie Publishing. Used by kind permission of Lancashire County Council Museum Service

exception of George V, who visited the town but declined to visit the castle. However, the Duchy's present Duke, Queen Elizabeth II, has made a record number of visits – in 1955, 1961, 1999 (to mark the 600th anniversary of the dukedom and crown coming together) and 2015 (to mark the 750th anniversary of the earldom). In addition, she has paid more attention to this county palatine than any Duke or monarch since Henry IV. While Queen Victoria insisted on keeping the title Queen of England on her visit, the present Queen is happy to be referred to as the Duke and was pleased when people attending Blackburn Cathedral sang 'God Save our Noble Duke' to her in 2014. Her last visit to Lancaster in 2015 was very similar to Queen Victoria's visit: it rained heavily just before she arrived, but cleared in time; the royal party arrived by train and travelled from the station to the castle gates (by car this time, Victoria went by carriage in 1851), and were shown the ceremonial keys of the castle by the Constable. However, Queen Victoria went on to view the courts, where a special throne, carved by Gillows of Lancaster, had been placed for her in the Shire Hall. This throne is now kept in the Grand Jury Room. Queen Elizabeth went on instead to see the former prison and meet members of the Duchy and castle staff. The plaque to commemorate her visit is in the gatehouse and clearly refers to her as: 'Queen Elizabeth, Duke of Lancaster'. Today, this is the loyal toast in the Palatinate of Lancaster, where she is the Palatinate's Duke and Queen. Therefore the Honour of Lancaster, with its castle founded in the 1090s, remains a part of the most powerful dukedom in the land – the sovereign's dukedom.

The plaque commemorating Queen Elizabeth II's visit to Lancaster Castle in 2015. Photograph by Colin Penny. Used by kind permission of the Duchy of Lancaster

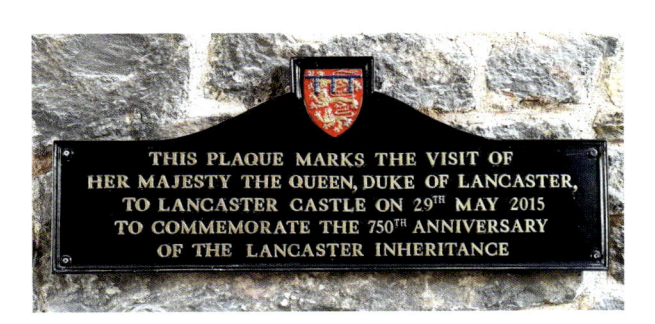

Lancaster Castle Assizes

The main event at Lancaster Castle in the years between 1200 and 1971 was the biannual County Assizes. The Assize courts were presided over by the monarch's personal judges, known as the King's Bench, who would be sent from London around the country for two months in the winter (February and March) and two months in the summer (July and August). Each county usually had one court for the Assizes, and for Lancashire this was situated solely at Lancaster Castle until 1835.

An Assize consisted of a minimum of two courts; one was the Crown Court, which oversaw criminal justice for serious crimes that could lead to loss of life or property. The other court of the Assize was the Court of Common Pleas, also known as the Civil Court. This was mainly for litigation cases between subjects of the realm and was based on an established civil right embodied in the Magna Carta. In addition, the Civil Court was also responsible for the regulation and enforcement of standard weights and measures in markets, shops and taverns.

Cases relating to more minor crimes, known as misdemeanours, were held at less important courts known as Quarter Sessions. In Lancashire these were held at Salford, Kirklees (Liverpool), Preston, Blackburn and Lancaster, but were known collectively as the 'Lancaster Quarter Sessions'. Those at Lancaster Castle were held from about 1361.

During the reign of King John (1199–1216), the civil court at Lancaster Castle was held in the keep. The criminal court was held then on the second floor of the Crown Building, which is where the Barristers' Library is located today. This is situated just above the Old

Cells that can be seen on the guided tour. Here, criminal justice was dispensed for over 600 years. In 1835, Liverpool broke Lancaster's monopoly and obtained the right to host its own Assizes for the south of the county, reducing Lancaster's remit to cover just the northern part of the county. The people of Lancaster were devastated at the news and, as the judges left Lancaster in 1835, all the church bells were tolled in mourning. Until then Lancaster was known as the 'Hanging Town' as only the Old Bailey in London sentenced more people to death. Public hangings were a big business and, in 1800, the town's population on hanging days could double from 8,000 to 16,000. It had been a major source of revenue for the town, but the loss of the south of the county to Liverpool in 1835 meant that no executions were held at Lancaster for the next 18 years.

In the 1790s two new courtrooms were built to replace the medieval ones. The grandest, the Civil Court, was completed in 1798 and is known today as the Shire Hall. In 1816 it was described in *The Times* as 'one of the most elegant spacious halls of justice in Great Britain', and today it represents one of the most magnificent Georgian buildings in England. The architect was a Yorkshireman, Thomas Harrison, and the first problem he had to overcome was the fact that he was building the Shire Hall on the site of the former castle moat, so the ground was quite soft. As a result, he had massive pillars sunk 20 feet into the ground to support the enormous weight

The Shire Hall. Photograph by Carnegie Publishing. Used by kind permission of Lancashire County Council Museum Service

of the structure he was building. On top of this he created a finely worked Georgian architectural masterpiece. The company Gillows of Lancaster, one of England's finest cabinetmakers, supplied the court furniture. In 1802, Joseph Gandy, one of the great names in Neo-Gothic architecture, designed the interior of the Hall, which included a magnificent frieze installed above the judge's bench. The style for the frieze is in the perpendicular gothic, which places the Shire Hall at the forefront of the gothic revival movement of the late eighteenth and early nineteenth centuries. The frieze is made of Coade Stone, a material invented by Eleanor Coade, consisting of a mixture of clay and glass that could be moulded. When baked it proves to be harder than many types of natural stone. Coade set up her factory on the South Bank in London and one of its most famous works is the stone lion on Westminster Bridge, although this was produced some years after her death. The frieze in the Shire Hall is the largest of her works produced for the north of England.

A hundred years ago it was decided to decorate the walls of the Shire Hall with a display of coats of arms, covering 800 years of the castle's history. All the monarchs are represented, from Richard I, along with the Constables of Lancaster Castle, and each High Sheriff of Lancashire. For the past 600 years the office of high sheriff has been an annual post, which explains the number of shields. Today, it is regarded as the largest public display of heraldry in the country. Each year a shield-hanging ceremony is held in the Shire Hall for the newly appointed high sheriff and their shield is added to the display.

Detail of the Coade Stone frieze above the judge's bench in the Shire Hall. Photograph by Carnegie Publishing. Used by kind permission of Lancashire County Council Museum Service

The largest public display of heraldry in the country. Photograph by Carnegie Publishing. Used by kind permission of Lancashire County Council Museum Service

The portrait of George III (1801) by James Northcote (1746–1831). Photograph by Carnegie Publishing. Used by kind permission of Lancashire County Council Museum Service

Across the corridor from the Shire Hall is the Crown Court, which was opened for use in 1795 during the reign of George III, and his portrait is above the judge's bench. This courtroom remains in use today and is one of the oldest serving crown courts in the country. In the dock can be seen the original eighteenth-century branding iron, which was used until 1811 to brand convicted criminals on the brawn of their left hand (below the thumb). The branding mark is a letter

47

The Crown Court. Photograph by Carnegie Publishing. Used by kind permission of Lancashire County Council Museum Service

'M' for Malefactor (a Latin legal term meaning 'evil-doer'). If, in the eighteenth century, a person wanted to show an employer that they did not have a criminal record, they would inform them that their 'hands were clean', whilst showing them their left hand. Equally, on the witness stand, to prove that a person was a reliable witness they would be asked to show a clean left palm to the jury while taking the oath. Branding was abolished in 1811, but Lancaster never removed its iron and clamp from the dock where it remains to this day. With the creation of the new Crown Court, the now redundant Crown Hall was remodeled and split into two, creating the Barristers' Robing Room and Library. The latter, which is now used as the jury waiting room, has an impressive plastered ceiling with a *trompe-l'œil* wood effect.

The right to hold the Assize court would have benefitted the town of Lancaster considerably. Every six months, court staff,

The original eighteenth-century branding iron, still in the dock today despite branding being abolished in 1811. Photograph by Carnegie Publishing. Used by kind permission of Lancashire County Council Museum Service

lawyers, their clients and witnesses would come to stay in the town, filling its inns. From the early seventeenth century, the judges stayed at the grandest house in Lancaster. Now known as the Judges' Lodgings, it was greatly enhanced in the early 1600s by Thomas Covell, who served as the gaoler at Lancaster Castle and was Mayor of Lancaster on six occasions. He was a self-made man, not unlike Thomas Cromwell, and he would host the judges on their arrival.

The library, now the jury waiting room, has an impressive plastered ceiling with a *trompe-l'œil* wood effect, shown to the right. Photograph by Colin Penny. Used by kind permission of Lancashire County Council Museum Service

The Judges' Lodgings, Lancaster, greatly enhanced in the early 1600s by Thomas Covell. Reproduced by kind permission of Lancashire County Council Museum Service

At the start of the Assizes the judges would parade from their lodgings up to the Priory Church, where a service would be held. The parade would then continue on to the courts – a display of pomp and circumstance that would draw in the crowds. However, the main draw at the Assizes would be the public executions that followed them. Before 1800 these were held on 'Golgotha Hill', somewhere near the site now occupied by Williamson Park. This was where the Pendle witches were hanged in 1612. However, with the improvements to the castle made in the 1790s, a new hanging spot was constructed, later known as the Hanging Corner. This was situated between the wall of a new two-storey round tower and the new curtain wall.

The upper floor of the tower was used as the Grand Jury Room. The Grand Jury consisted of 13 to 24 men of high standing (socially and politically speaking), who would examine the evidence against the accused prior to a trial in the Crown Court in front of the Petty Jury. They would look at the paperwork and interview witnesses. If they felt that there was sufficient evidence for a trial, they would then hand their decision over to the judge in court and the trial would proceed. In about 1803, the room was furnished by Gillows of Lancaster, with a set of unique chairs, each of which incorporating a one-off carved head. Another seven chairs were added later, all bearing carved cherub heads, as was the large oak table. The Grand Jury system continued in the United Kingdom until

Hanging Corner. Photograph by Carnegie Publishing. Used by kind permission of Lancashire County Council Museum Service

The Grand Jury Room, the witness box and judges' chairs by Gillows of Lancaster, and below, details of Gillows chairs. Photographs by Carnegie Publishing. Used by kind permission of Lancashire County Council Museum Service

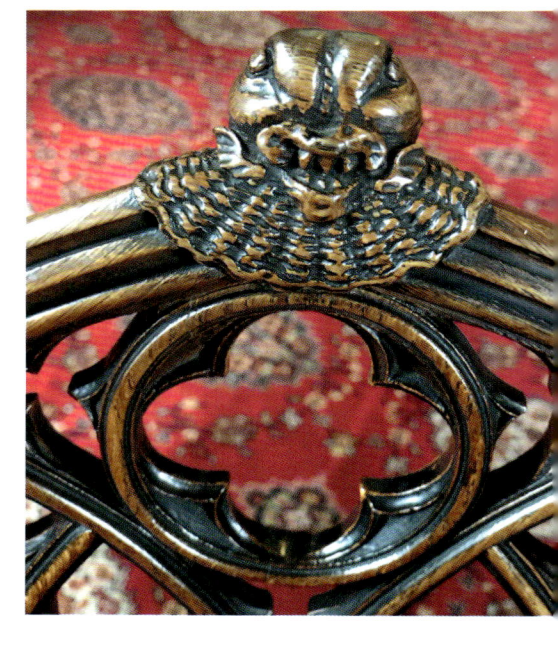

The Drop Room. Photograph by Colin Penny. Used by kind permission of Lancashire County Council Museum Service

The Pinioning Strap. Photograph by Colin Penny. Used by kind permission of Lancashire County Council Museum Service

1933, being replaced by the Crown Prosecution Service, after which the Grand Jury Room was no longer used for that purpose.

The lower floor contained the Drop Room, where the condemned were prepared for the gallows, having been taken there from the Prison Chapel where they had been given the opportunity to pray. The Drop Room was used for the first time in 1800. Here they were prepared for execution by being pinioned and were often given a drink to help calm their nerves. At noon, the 'Death Bell' would toll and the door leading from the Drop Room would open – the prisoner would then emerge to the waiting crowds. Another use of the Drop Room was to keep the hangman and his assistant dry for the hour that had to elapse between a person being hanged and their body being cut down. At the end of an hour they would go back out onto the gallows, cut the rope and take the body back inside. At midnight, the executed person having been certified dead by the prison doctor, the coffin containing their body would

At noon, the 'Death Bell' would toll and the prisoner would emerge to the waiting crowds. Photograph by Carnegie Publishing. Used by kind permission of Lancashire County Council Museum Service

A 'short drop' noose said to have been used for the execution of Stephen Burke in 1865. Photograph by Carnegie Publishing. Used by kind permission of Lancashire County Council Museum Service

be lowered through a trap door from the Drop Room to the ground below. Until 1832, most of those executed at Hanging Corner were buried under what is now the court car park; in the case of murderers, however, doctors could claim their bodies for medical dissection. One of the doctors who did such work was the prison assistant surgeon, Dr Richard Owen, who later became known as the 'dinosaur man'.

For the majority of those hanged, a public execution resulted in a slow death by strangulation and this was known as the 'short drop' method due to the very short length of rope used. In 1868 public executions were abolished and thereafter hangings at Lancaster were carried out in the privacy of the prison. The number of executions also declined rapidly, with only seven taking place between 1868 and 1887, and these being carried out in what is now called Chapel Yard. The final execution at Lancaster, that of Thomas Rawcliffe in 1910, was carried out in a purpose-built 'topping shed' in what would become known as the Execution Yard. The method used in these later executions was the 'long drop' method, where the snapping of the condemned's neck would kill them instantly.

If a convicted person's crime was serious, but did not warrant the death penalty, then the alternative was usually transportation overseas. Convicts would usually be transported for periods of seven years, fourteen years or for life. During this time male prisoners worked as convict labour, and undertook activities such as roadbuilding, felling trees, working in sawmills, brickmaking, agricultural work, etc. Women were usually assigned to roles in domestic service, factories or laundries. At the end of their sentence, or earlier if they had been well-behaved, these convicts would be given their 'ticket of leave', and if they were not serving a life sentence they were free and allowed to return home. The problem for many, though, was that the British government did

The 'topping shed' in Execution Yard. This has since been removed. Reproduced by kind permission of Lancashire County Council Museum Service

not pay for their return – they had to find the fare themselves, and the vast majority were never able to do so. As a result, most transportees never returned home. That said, a large number did not want to return to Britain, having started new lives for themselves in a 'land of opportunity'. Convicts who were sentenced to life would also receive a ticket of leave after a period of time, usually around 10 to 15 years. These convicts, however, were never allowed to return home even if they could afford to. If they did, and were captured, the sentence for doing so was death.

Transportation began in 1597 and was generally to the American colonies until their Declaration of Independence in 1776. During the War of Independence, Britain kept its criminals awaiting transportation on old 'hulks' – disused warships that were beached along the south coast of Britain and used as makeshift prisons. However, after the war, despite the willingness of Britain to continue sending her convicts to the United States, the new republic refused to accept them. So, from 1788, many criminals convicted of serious or repeat offences were transported to Australia instead. Two Lancaster children were among those on board the very first fleet – these were Elizabeth and George Youngson. In fact, Lancaster Crown Court sentenced so many convicts to transportation that it would establish a strong link between the castle and the beginning of Australia's European settlement. In recognition of this, the castle has since established a major database for the many Australian family history enquiries received from descendants of those transported. Transportation came to an end in 1868.

In 1971 the Assize courts were abolished and a new three-tier system was established. Lancaster's courts were then downgraded to third-division courts. However, Lancaster's Crown Court, in all of its eighteenth-century majesty, remains architecturally one of the most magnificent courtrooms in the United Kingdom.

Prisoners of Religious Conscience

Lancaster Castle has become a place of religious pilgrimage, particularly for Roman Catholics and Quakers. In 2016 every Catholic primary school within the Diocese of Lancaster made a pilgrimage to honour the Lancashire Martyrs, who were tried at the castle and executed on the moor overlooking the city. From all over the world Quakers make the journey to Lancaster Castle to see the place where both George Fox and Margaret Fell, the founders of the Quaker movement, were tried in 1664, and where so many other Lancashire Quakers were imprisoned and died for their faith.

The first of Lancashire's Catholic martyrdoms occurred during the reign of Henry VIII (1509–47). Henry's break with Rome was not initially an English Protestant revolution, but an attempt by Henry to establish an independent English Catholic Church. However, in seizing the properties of the church, particularly the monasteries, he saw a chance to enrich himself and his followers – the result was the Dissolution of the Monasteries. Not surprisingly, this proved very unpopular with many people, and there was great opposition to Henry's religious policies in the north of England. One manifestation of this was the so-called Pilgrimage of Grace, which was intended to be a peaceful protest. Henry viewed such demonstrations, however, as rebellion, and those involved as no more than traitors. Two of those arrested following the Pilgrimage of Grace were John Paslew, the Abbot of Whalley Abbey, and fellow monk, William Haydock. Both were condemned for the crime of treason:

Paslew was executed at Lancaster on 10 March 1536, while Haydock was taken back to the abbey where he was hanged. Whalley Abbey was then dissolved and its lands sold.

England's real move towards becoming a Protestant state came during reign of Henry's son, Edward VI (1547–53), however Edward died young , before his religious policies could be established. Mary, his Catholic sister, succeeded him and attempted to reverse her brother's work by returning England to the Roman Catholic Church. Some of those who opposed her religious policies, such as the Archbishop of Canterbury, Thomas Cranmer, were burnt at the stake, and one Lancashire preacher who refused to give up his Protestant faith was George Marsh. George came from Deane, near Bolton, where he was born in 1515. He was arrested in 1554 and was held at Lancaster Castle for a year. Here he read the Bible out loud to his fellow prisoners, and preached from his window to listeners in the street below. In order that the people below could hear him, it is probable that he was held in one of the lower rooms of the gatehouse. He became too popular with the townsfolk for the authorities to tolerate and so, in 1555, he was moved to Chester. There he was asked to recant and, when he refused, he was burnt at the stake on 24 April. Memorials to him can be seen at Chester and Deane.

Following Mary's death in 1558, the country shifted again towards Protestantism, under Mary's sister Elizabeth I (1558–1603). She was aware, however, that many of her subjects held Catholic beliefs. As a result, she established a compromise – that a man or woman could hold any religious belief they wished to in England so long as they attended an Anglican church every Sunday and followed Anglican services. Catholics, who refused this, and held their own services, were known as recusant Catholics. They faced heavy fines or imprisonment, but not execution, and some known recusant Catholics still held public office, for example the Dukes of Norfolk. The situation was different, however, for the Catholic priesthood, especially after 1570 when the pope excommunicated Elizabeth I as a heretic. This created a situation whereby it became the duty of all Catholics to rebel against her, and such an action would not be regarded as a sin. This could also be perceived by some as an encouragement to assassinate her. The result was that the monarch and government began to regard her Catholic subjects with deep suspicion. Priests coming into the country from abroad to attend to English Catholics were regarded as foreign agents of the pope, sent to stir up rebellion and to overthrow the legitimate Protestant government of England. They were viewed as owing their allegiance to the pope, and not to the king or queen of England. In this light they were regarded as traitors to the crown, and so would face a traitor's death – to be hung, drawn and quartered. This was an especially savage punishment which involved the condemned being drawn to the place of execution on a hurdle behind a horse. They were then strung up by the neck until they were near the point of death, before being cut down and butchered alive. Their heads and the four quarters of their body were then displayed as a warning to all other traitors. Anyone found to be hiding priests faced death by hanging. Between 1557 and 1679, over 40 priests and their supporters were executed for treason in England and they are collectively known as the English Catholic Martyrs. A quarter of them were tried at Lancaster Castle, as Lancashire at the time was the most Catholic county in England. Lancashire had never participated fully in the Protestant Reformation and many of its leading landed families remained Catholic, whether openly or secretly. As a major centre of English Catholicism, the county attracted more priests than many other parts of the country and, as a result, a large number were captured here.

One of these priests was James Bell, who was born in Warrington and executed at Lancaster in 1584. He had become a Catholic priest during the reign of Mary I, but on the accession of Elizabeth I, had been converted to Anglicanism. In 1581, after 20 years of working as a Protestant preacher, he returned to the Catholic fold. He was subsequently arrested and tried for treason, being executed on 10 April 1584. He was executed alongside a yeoman farmer, John Finch, who had been raised as a Protestant but converted to Catholicism. He had helped to conceal travelling priests in his home, but was betrayed and arrested by the Earl of Derby. He was imprisoned and tortured for three years before being tried and executed.

Richard Blundell of Little Crosby was imprisoned, along with his son, William, at Lancaster Castle in 1590 for his Catholic faith. Both were still imprisoned at the castle two years later when Richard died of natural causes. They had been arrested alongside a seminary priest, named as Mr Woodroffe. William stated that other Catholics were imprisoned in the castle at the same time, including Richard Worthington, who also died in the prison. William Blundell spent five years in the castle before he was released.

In 1600, Robert Nutter, a priest from East Lancashire, was executed in Lancaster. In 1584 he and his brother were arrested in London and severely tortured. Although Robert was spared, he had to watch his brother's execution, and was afterwards exiled from England. He returned in 1585 but was re-arrested and imprisoned for the next 15 years. In March 1600 he managed to escape from Wisbech Castle, but was caught and sent north to Lancaster. He was executed on 26 July. Robert was the brother-in-law of Alice Nutter of Roughlee, who was one of the Pendle witches tried at the castle in 1612. Edward Thwing, despite his ill health, had served Lancashire as a priest for three years before being caught and he was executed alongside Robert Nutter in 1600.

In 1601, Robert Middleton from York was executed. He was another former Protestant who had converted to the Catholic faith and his sister admonished him at his execution to recant. She even promised to pay £100 to any Anglican minster who would try to convert him back to the Protestant faith. This would have saved him – the authorities preferred the propaganda victory of a priest recanting his faith than one dying a martyr's death – but Middleton refused. Alongside him on the scaffold was Thurston Hunt, a priest who had been arrested when he tried to save Middleton on the latter's way to Lancaster. He had served the Catholics of Lancashire for 15 years, and when arrested he was found to have a letter addressed to Elizabeth I warning her of a plot by the Earl of Essex. He was sent to London and questioned, but this did not save him – he was returned to Lancaster, tried and executed. In 1604, Lawrence Bailey was hanged for assisting priests.

At about this time a ballad was written and sung throughout the county to honour some of these men:

Amongst this gracious group that follow Christ his train
To cause the Devil stoop, four priest were lately slain
Nutter's bold constancy with his sweet fellow Thwing
Of whose most meek modesty angels and saint may sing

Hunt's haughty courage stout with godly zeal so true
Mild Middleton, oh what tongue can half thy virtue show
At Lancaster lovingly these martyrs took their end
In glorious victory true faith for to defend

A year later the priest John Thules was arrested at the Chorley house of Robert Wrenno, a 'poor weaver'. He and Robert escaped during the night from the castle but, by sunrise, they found they had wandered in a circle and were back outside their prison where they were immediately re-arrested. After watching the brutal execution of Thules, Wrenno was then strung up, but his rope broke. The high sheriff cried to him: 'Look, it is God's will thou should not die, take the oath therefore and be a good subject and the King will show you mercy'. Wrenno replied, 'If you had seen that which I have just now seen, you would be in as much haste to die as I now am'.

In 1628, Lancaster witnessed the execution of the town's most famous Catholic Martyr, Edmund Arrowsmith. He was born in Haydock in 1585 and his family had suffered much for their faith. His grandfather had been imprisoned and his parents heavily fined for not attending Anglican services. Then the authorities

Stained glass window depicting the Blessed Robert Wrenno, with the broken rope around his neck. Copyright St Mary's Church, Chorley

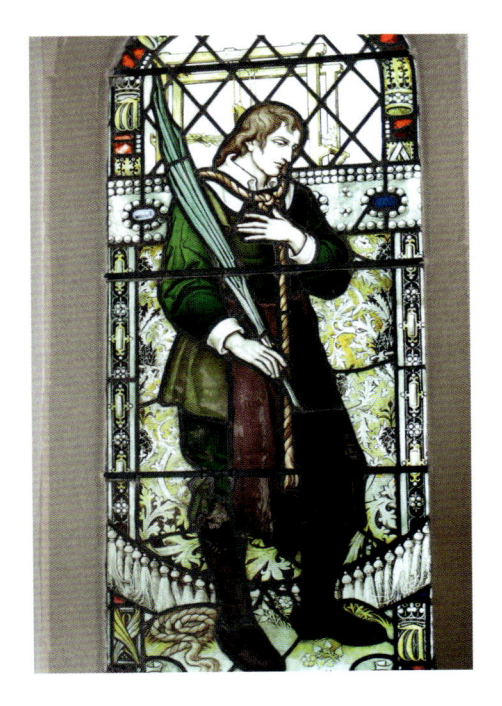

Stained glass window depicting St Ambrose Barlow. Copyright: The Cathedral Church of St John the Evangelist, Salford

decided that his parents were holding secret masses with a priest and raided their house. It was searched thoroughly, but they failed to find anyone. Not content, they bound Edmund's parents and took them to Lancaster Castle, leaving Edmund and his three younger siblings freezing in the night air outside their locked house. The neighbours rescued them, but these early experiences left an indelible mark on Edmund. As a young man, he left England in 1605 to train as a priest at the English College of Douai in Flanders. He was ordained in 1612 and, in 1613, returned to attend to the Catholics of south Lancashire. He was arrested nine years later and brought before the Bishop of Chester, in front of whom he is said to have argued his position so effectively that he was released. 1622 also witnessed a general amnesty, issued by James I, to all imprisoned Catholic priests, and it is quite likely that this also played a large part in the circumstances leading to his release. However, in 1628 Edmund sought to help a young man who had 'fallen from God', whom he reproached for his incestuous marriage with his cousin. The young man and his mother resented this, and betrayed Edmund to the authorities.

The judge at the trial, Sir Henry Yelverton, took a strong disliking to the fierce Edmund and asked him whether he was a priest. Edmund cleverly replied, 'I would to God I were worthy'. Yelverton then harangued him and Edmund offered to defend his faith in court, but this was something Yelverton was not prepared to allow. Edmund then replied that he was happy to defend his creed, not only with his words, but with his blood. The judge was furious and replied, 'You shall seal it with your blood!' and took sadistic pleasure in describing the execution that awaited him, vowing not to leave Lancaster until he had seen the deed done. Edmund coolly replied: 'And you too, my Lord, must die'. After the sentence had been passed Edmund knelt and said 'Deo gratias, God be thanked'. The judge then ordered Edmund to be chained, and held in a tiny, dark, cell – a 'cell of little ease'. The cell was shaped like an anvil, where he could neither stand up nor lie down in comfort, and even sitting caused great discomfort. A cell of this description exists in Hadrian's Tower and many believe that this was Edmund Arrowsmith's final cell.

On 29 August 1628 Edmund was laid down on the hurdle and dragged across the town to the place of his execution, which is believed to be the field next to where St Peter's Catholic Cathedral now stands today. As he stood on the scaffold, an appeal by an Anglican priest to recant received the reply: 'Good sir, tempt me not. The mercy which I look for lies in heaven, through the death and Passion of my Saviour Jesus'. He pulled his hat over his eyes and plunged, his last words being: 'Bone Jesus (O Good Jesus)'.

Richard Hurst, a farmer, was hanged alongside Edmund Arrowsmith. He had originally been arrested for aiding a priest, but, while resisting arrest, he broke the leg of one of the arresting officers, who later died. Hurst was convicted both for aiding a priest and for murder.

In 1641, one of the saintliest of Lancashire's priests was executed, this was Ambrose Barlow who came from Manchester. He had worked as a priest in the county since 1617 and at his trial the judge was amazed by the bravery and consistency of Barlow's replies. He reminded Ambrose that his life was in his hands by saying, 'don't you know and acknowledge that I sit here as your judge?' But Barlow replied that he was a judge only in temporal matters, but in the spiritual and that of conscience, he, Barlow, was the judge: 'I tell you plainly that if by that unjust law you sentence me to die, it will to be to my salvation and your damnation'. When the judge passed the death sentence, Barlow said he would pray to God to forgive the judge and the jury. Hearing such charity, the judge was moved to ensure that Barlow would spend his last night in the comfort of the castle chambers, rather than in a cell. Barlow died the next day, firm in his faith.

In 1646, the last of Lancaster's Catholic martyrs were executed. These were: Edward Bamber of Poulton-le-Fylde; the Franciscan priest, John Woodcock of Leyland; and Thomas Whittaker of St Michael's on the Wyre. Bamber was remembered for throwing money to the crowd and giving absolution to a murderer who was to be hanged with him. Woodcock was strung up but the rope broke, but in this instance he was not given the opportunity to save himself. The young Thomas Whittaker (born in 1611) was saved until last, and he looked on, terrified, at the brutal execution of his fellow priests. The authorities deliberately left this scared and nervous young man to the last, sensing that he might recant rather than face the fate of his fellow priests. But, when offered to do so, he replied: 'Use your pleasure with me. A reprieve or even a pardon upon your condition I utterly refuse,' and he climbed up to be hanged and executed. They say true bravery comes when you are most afraid.

The seventeenth century was not the last time that Catholic priests were arrested in Lancashire for suspected treason. Following the 1745 Jacobite Rebellion, strong anti-Catholic feelings arose in the county and priests again became suspect in their loyalty to the crown. Father John Sergeant was arrested for having met Bonnie Prince Charlie and was imprisoned at the castle. While at the Catholic mission of Lee House, a mob broke in and seized Father Germaine Helme as a possible Jacobite supporter. Later Sergeant was released, but Helme died while imprisoned at the castle, poisoned according to the accounts by an unknown 'malicious woman'. Was he the last of the county's Catholic martyrs?

In the twentieth century all but one of these martyrs were beatified, that is to be known as 'The Blessed'; the exception being Lawrence Bailey who remained 'Most Venerable'. Edmund

Arrowsmith and Ambrose Barlow were later canonised as saints in 1970. At the Catholic parish church of St Mary's in Little Crosby, north Liverpool, there is a stained glass window dedicated to Edmund Arrowsmith, and a stained glass window in Lancaster Cathedral also commemorates him. Following his execution Edmund's hand was preserved as a relic at the Church of St Oswald in Ashton-in-Makerfield. Later, a plaque to commemorate all of the Martyrs was placed on the wall of Lancaster Castle gatehouse, the place where their heads would have been displayed following their execution.

Under Elizabeth I's broad Anglican church, dissent came not just from those of the Catholic faith, but also from those who felt that the Anglican church had not become Protestant enough.

A plaque to commemorate the Roman Catholic Martyrs, situated on the wall of Lancaster Castle gatehouse, where their heads would have been displayed following their execution. Photograph by Graham Kemp. Used by kind permission of the Duchy of Lancaster

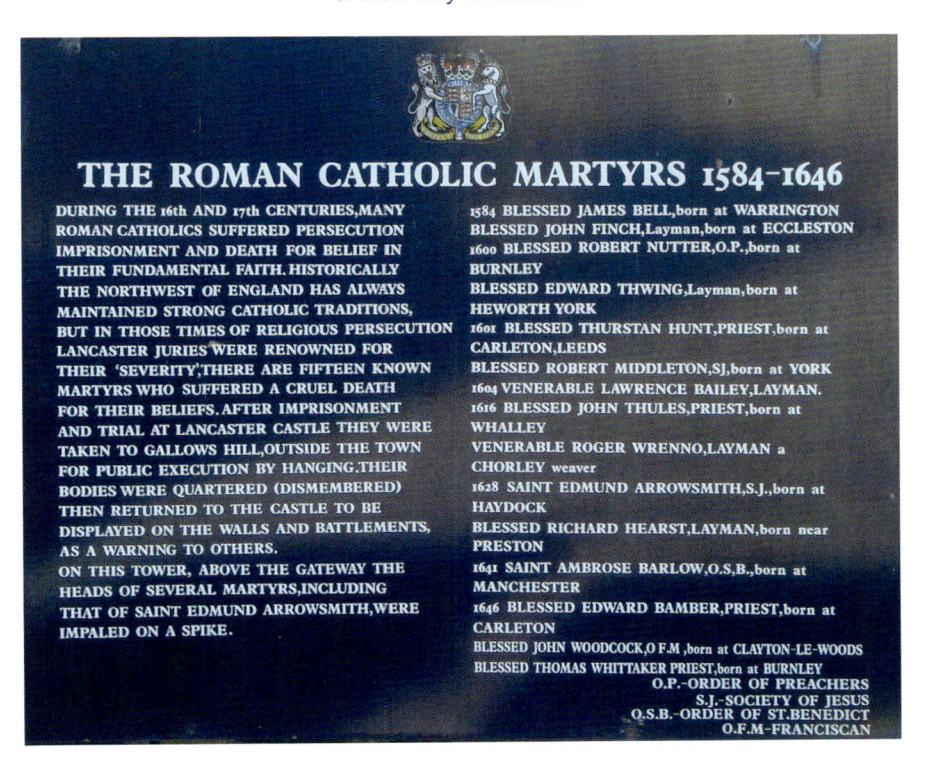

THE ROMAN CATHOLIC MARTYRS 1584-1646

DURING THE 16th AND 17th CENTURIES, MANY ROMAN CATHOLICS SUFFERED PERSECUTION IMPRISONMENT AND DEATH FOR BELIEF IN THEIR FUNDAMENTAL FAITH. HISTORICALLY THE NORTHWEST OF ENGLAND HAS ALWAYS MAINTAINED STRONG CATHOLIC TRADITIONS, BUT IN THOSE TIMES OF RELIGIOUS PERSECUTION LANCASTER JURIES WERE RENOWNED FOR THEIR 'SEVERITY'. THERE ARE FIFTEEN KNOWN MARTYRS WHO SUFFERED A CRUEL DEATH FOR THEIR BELIEFS. AFTER IMPRISONMENT AND TRIAL AT LANCASTER CASTLE THEY WERE TAKEN TO GALLOWS HILL, OUTSIDE THE TOWN FOR PUBLIC EXECUTION BY HANGING. THEIR BODIES WERE QUARTERED (DISMEMBERED) THEN RETURNED TO THE CASTLE TO BE DISPLAYED ON THE WALLS AND BATTLEMENTS, AS A WARNING TO OTHERS.
ON THIS TOWER, ABOVE THE GATEWAY THE HEADS OF SEVERAL MARTYRS, INCLUDING THAT OF SAINT EDMUND ARROWSMITH, WERE IMPALED ON A SPIKE.

1584 BLESSED JAMES BELL, born at WARRINGTON
BLESSED JOHN FINCH, Layman, born at ECCLESTON
1600 BLESSED ROBERT NUTTER, O.P., born at BURNLEY
BLESSED EDWARD THWING, Layman, born at HEWORTH YORK
1601 BLESSED THURSTAN HUNT, PRIEST, born at CARLETON, LEEDS
BLESSED ROBERT MIDDLETON, SJ, born at YORK
1604 VENERABLE LAWRENCE BAILEY, LAYMAN.
1616 BLESSED JOHN THULES, PRIEST, born at WHALLEY
VENERABLE ROGER WRENNO, LAYMAN a CHORLEY weaver
1628 SAINT EDMUND ARROWSMITH, S.J., born at HAYDOCK
BLESSED RICHARD HEARST, LAYMAN, born near PRESTON
1641 SAINT AMBROSE BARLOW, O.S.B., born at MANCHESTER
1646 BLESSED EDWARD BAMBER, PRIEST, born at CARLETON
BLESSED JOHN WOODCOCK, O.F.M, born at CLAYTON-LE-WOODS
BLESSED THOMAS WHITTAKER PRIEST, born at BURNLEY
O.P.-ORDER OF PREACHERS
S.J.-SOCIETY OF JESUS
O.S.B.-ORDER OF ST.BENEDICT
O.F.M-FRANCISCAN

These dissenters wanted a more 'pure' and simple faith and were commonly known as Puritans. As the seventeenth century progressed, these dissenters fragmented into a number of sects and many were persecuted. However, unlike the Catholic Martyrs, they were not perceived as agents of a foreign power, so they did not face a traitor's death if arrested for their beliefs. They were non-conformists to the Anglican church and so they were fined, imprisoned and harassed. Many avoided persecution by going to America. A member of the Lancashire Standish family, Myles Standish, captained the Mayflower in 1621, taking the Pilgrim Fathers to the New World.

In the 1640s, for one young man, the non-conformists were not practising purely enough. He announced that he had received a vision from God on Pendle Hill, and began to preach a very simple creed. This was George Fox and, when he was arraigned before a magistrate for 'religious blasphemy', he told the magistrate to tremble in the sight of the Lord. The magistrate replied jokingly

George Fox. Reproduced by kind permission of Swarthmoor Hall

Swathmoor Hall, near Ulverston, home of Thomas Fell. Reproduced by kind permission of Swarthmoor Hall

that Fox made him 'quake', and thus Fox's followers became known as the Quakers. Another, less likely, origin for the name is said to derive from the physical quaking which members of the movement manifested during their religious experience. One of Fox's early converts was Margaret Fell, the wife of Thomas Fell of Swathmoor Hall, near Ulverston. Thomas Fell was a high court judge and Vice Chancellor of the Duchy of Lancaster, and he gave Fox protection to pursue his preaching. He needed it, as he had created many enemies; for example, on one occasion he was driven from Lancaster Priory Church and stoned along the streets of Lancaster for his preaching. When Thomas Fell died in 1658, Fox's enemies were quick to act against him. He was arrested in 1660 and was freed thanks to Margaret Fell's personal intervention with the newly restored King Charles II. Fox left Lancashire for a few years, but on his return to Swarthmoor in 1663 he was again arrested, this time with Margaret Fell. They were taken to Lancaster Castle, and kept in appalling conditions for six months until the Assizes of March 1664.

George complained bitterly about his prison cell, in which he said the wind and the rain came from above, and the smoke from below – he described his cell as his 'dark house'. Although not certain, it is probable that this was situated in the Dungeon Tower. In the early nineteenth century it was said of this tower that when in the morning the gaoler opened the door to it, he had to wait 15 minutes before entering due to the stench. Margaret was also kept in a dungeon at Lancaster Castle. The judge, knowing her connections through her deceased husband, hoped he could persuade her through such confinement to be more compliant and less of a professional embarrassment to him. He was wrong. Margaret gave a formidable and spirited defence, even persuading the judge and the high sheriff to view where she had been kept and apologise to her for its dreadful condition. Finally, however, she and George were convicted, and to ensure George Fox was no further trouble in the county he was sent to Scarborough, in Yorkshire, to serve his time. Margaret was sentenced to life, and was kept at Lancaster Castle. In 1668 through her tireless efforts she got an order from the king for her release and on gaining her freedom married George Fox. Margaret is known as the mother of Quakerism, and it was through her efforts that the Quaker movement became one of the few Christian sects at this time to value women in their own right as agents of religion.

The Quakers' Room, the name of the dining room at the new debtors block. engraving by Thomas Physick, after drawing by Edward Slack. Reproduced by kind permission of Lancaster City Museum

Many other Quakers were arrested during the sixteenth and early seventeenth centuries and imprisoned at Lancaster, usually for refusing to pay their tithes (a tax to the Anglican church). They tended to be held in the keep, on the right-hand side of the second floor as one faces it from the Chapel Yard, and the room was known for a long time afterwards as the Quakers' Room. In the late seventeenth century it became the residence of many of the debtors imprisoned at the castle and, when a new debtors' block was built between 1794 and 1796 (today's B-Wing), the debtors named their dining room, the Quakers' Room. Some Quakers were also held in the 'Oven Tower' which is today called Hadrian's Tower. Although not executed for their beliefs, many suffered terrible punishments during their stay, and a significant number died of disease. The last Quaker to die at the castle was John Haydock in 1720. The Quaker poetess, Mary Southworth (later Mollineax), was also kept at the castle, and wrote the poem 'Meditations Concerning Our Imprisonment, only for Conscience-Sake', 1684, in Lancaster Castle.

As Quakers allowed their women to preach, the women suffered a particularly cruel punishment for their 'audacity'. In Hadrian's Tower there are two Scold's Bridles, and these were used for punishing outspoken and gossiping women. Each consists of a metal cage placed over the head, with a tongue piece (the bridle) that went into the mouth to rest on the tongue. Those subjected to this punishment were dragged around the market-place, often backwards, for an hour in the morning and an hour in the afternoon to be publicly humiliated. Some towns put mustard on the 'bridle' and others even spikes. If they slipped while wearing this, they often broke their teeth, sometimes even their jaw. The cruelty of this device was intended to put women in their 'place', and since a woman preaching religion was regarded as an offence to God in the eyes of the seventeenth-century Anglican Church, many good Quaker women suffered this punishment.

By the end of the eighteenth century, prisoners of religious conscience had mostly become a thing of the past. In 1760, the Quaker William Butterfield became the Constable of the castle

A scold's bridle, used for punishing outspoken and gossiping women
Reproduced by kind permission of Lancashire County Council Museum Service

and, 60 years later, Elizabeth Fry would come to the prison, but as a prison reformer rather than as a Quaker prisoner. Yet, more than a century later, some Quakers would return to the castle due to their beliefs. Between 1943 and 1945, Quakers, along with members of the Plymouth Brethren and Jehovah's Witnesses, were made to reside in the castle as conscientious objectors. Serving in the Non-Combatant Corps, they were not prisoners, but neither were they really free.

The Lancashire Witches: 1612

On 13 March 1612, a pedlar from Halifax was travelling along the road to Colne, a market town which lay at the foot of the great hill of Pendle; this pedlar's name was John Law. As he neared the town a young beggar girl approached and asked if he would give her some pins. Regarding her as a nuisance, John Law refused, and an altercation took place between them. At that time, if a beggar was refused, it was traditional for them to 'curse their mark' to make them feel uncomfortable and perhaps to help change their mind. It seems that this girl cursed Law as he walked away and, probably to her surprise, he suddenly collapsed before her. Horrified, she ran off. This was the incident that would lead to one of the most infamous witchcraft trials in English history: the Lancashire Witch Trials of 1612.

The girl, Alison Device, lived in Pendle Forest, lying to the west of the great hill itself. A 'forest' was not originally a wooded area, but a fenced off region reserved for the king's deer. In these areas the king and his retinue would hunt. Alison's last name was probably not Device, but Davies. However, to a Londoner, the name 'Davies' when pronounced with an East Lancashire dialect, sounds like Dev-ies, or Dev-ICE, and the writer of the original account of the trials was a Londoner. Alison belonged to a family at the bottom of society who survived by doing odd jobs or by begging and stealing where necessary. They were dominated by an old matriarch, who was descended from a long line of thieves and brigands. Her name was Mrs Southern, but she was also known as 'Old Demdyke', a seventeenth-century term for a 'demon woman'. To protect her family, she may have used the 'threat of being a witch' to put fear into others. By 1612, however, she was blind, and Alison, when not working as a beggar, cared for her and acted as her eyes. She was known as her 'grandmother's blessing' and would often be seen leading Southern around the forest.

Alison also lived with her mother, Southern's daughter, Elizabeth – who was known as 'Squinting Lizzie'. In addition there was her brother, James, and her younger sister Jennet – the identity of their father remains unknown. She also had an uncle, Southern's son, Christopher Holgate. The family lived in Malkin Tower, a grand-sounding name for a property which was almost certainly a hovel.

Returning to John Law; following his collapse, he was found by the roadside. He had become paralysed down his left side, his face had fallen, and he was unable to speak. It is clear to us now that he may have suffered a stroke and it was not Alison's curse which had caused his illness. However, to those who looked on in the seventeenth century it appeared to be a witch's hex. He was taken to Colne and, two days later, his son, Abraham, arrived to take him back to Halifax. At this point the whole affair may have ended had Alison not turned up to apologise for her curse. It is said that John Law tried to communicate his forgiveness, but his son would not have any of it. Seeing her as a witch he dragged her to the local magistrate, Roger Nowell of Reed Hall. Roger was an experienced barrister of nearly 40 years, an ex-high sheriff of Lancashire, and a few years before he had prosecuted a witch at Lancaster Castle – the tutor of his nephew's children. He regarded himself as an expert in the judicial prosecution of witches. He questioned Alison, and as an experienced barrister he soon interpreted the simple and naïve Alison's words as further proof of her guilt. She also, unwittingly, managed to implicate her grandmother and one of their neighbours as well.

On 30 March, Nowell interrogated Alison's grandmother, Mrs Southern, and her neighbour, Anne Whittle. Here, he had struck gold, as the two women hated each other and both were happy to implicate the other. On the evidence of Southern he also arrested Whittle's daughter, Ann Redfearn. Later, he heard news of a major meeting at Malkin Tower due to take place on Good Friday

(20 April), which included another suspected witch called Jennet Preston. Roger Nowell decided this meant that the meeting had to be a witches' sabbat and that he was in the process of uncovering an entire coven of witches. Jennet Preston came from Gisburn, which lies just across the Yorkshire border from Pendle. In fact, Jennet was only 'guilty' of being a friend of a Thomas Lister, who had cried out her name when he had suddenly died at his son's wedding in front of the guests and his wife. Mrs Lister and the family immediately started a campaign against Jennet to see her convicted and hanged as a witch. At the Lent Assizes in York, the judge, Sir Edward Bromley, dismissed the case against her – he did not believe in witchcraft. But the Lister family did not give up and, the following July, finally had her convicted by a different judge, Lord Altham, following which she was hanged. Both Bromley and Altham would play a further part in this story.

There had been up to 20 people at the meeting on Good Friday, but Roger Nowell only caught seven of them – five women and two men. Mr Bulcock and his mother, who claimed they were not even there, but who were perhaps present as the 'caterers'. They had supplied a stolen sheep which was cooked and eaten. Interestingly, sheep stealing was itself a hanging offence, and much easier to prove that witchcraft, but the authorities were not interested in such a run-of-the-mill offence. The other man arrested was Alison's brother, James, who was betrayed to the authorities by his supposed friend, Mr Hargreaves, the constable.

With these seven, Nowell had altogether arrested 11 witches from Pendle and sent them all to Lancaster to be tried at the next Assizes to be held in August. The 11 were:

From the Southern Family of Malkin Tower:

> Mrs Southern (Old Demdyke)
> Elizabeth Device (Squinting Lizzie)
> James Device
> Alison Device

From the Whittle Family (neighbours of Mrs Southern):

Ann Whittle (nicknamed Old Chattox)
Ann Redfearn (Ann Whittle's daughter)

Others arrested for attending the so-called sabbat:

Katherine Hewitt (nicknamed Mould Heels)
Alice Gray (Katherine's friend)
Alice Nutter of Roughlea
John Bulcock
Jane Bulcock (John's mother)

The 'witches' were possibly kept in the dungeon below the Well Tower, and it may have been here that Southern died before the trial. At the Assizes in August 1612, the charges against the accused had escalated considerably. They faced none other than Sir Edward Bromley, the witchcraft sceptic, with Lord Altham acting as the supporting judge. Although Altham may have been sympathetic towards Mr Nowell's cause, Nowell would still have had his work cut out with the sceptical Bromley who would preside

The Well Tower dungeon, where the witches are believed to have been held. Photograph by Colin Penny. Used by kind permission of the Duchy of Lancaster

over the case. The evidence supplied was mostly hearsay, along with some confessions which were dubious and contradictory. For example, Anne Whittle was charged with the murder by witchcraft of Robert Nutter 20 years previously, but she had confessed to being a witch for only the past 14 years. As a good judge, Bromley should have spotted this contradiction, but he did not – or perhaps he chose to ignore it. James's confession seemed to have been beaten out of him. He had arrived at the castle a fit man, but, when in the dock, he was barely able to walk or talk, and little of his confession made sense. Bromley would have known that a confession produced under torture was inadmissible in an English court without the king's expressed sanction, a fact enshrined in the Magna Carta. Again, Bromley overlooked it. Anne Whittle's daughter, Ann Redfearn, was found not guilty by the jury for the murder of Robert Nutter but was brought back the next day to be tried for the murder of Robert Nutter's father on the evidence of two witnesses. One of these was now dead and the other was described by Nowell himself as unreliable. Again Bromley ignored these facts, and Ann was convicted. So what exactly was going on?

The answer lies in the fact that in 1612 Lancashire was the most Catholic county in England, with many of its leading houses being either actively or secretly Catholic – even the high sheriff of that year was a leading Catholic. King James I (1603–25), however, did not trust English Catholics, although this was not simply an issue of religion. James himself was a Protestant, but he was married to a Catholic convert. It was more to do with the Gunpowder Plot and the fact that some English Catholics had tried to blow him up on 5 November 1605. Lancashire's leading Catholics had nothing to do with the plot – in fact one of them, Lord Monteagle, had even supplied the anonymous letter that warned the government of the plot. However, James was still deeply distrustful of all English Catholics after these events. It was possible that the Lancashire Catholic gentry were looking for some means to regain the king's trust.

When James came to England in 1603, he discovered that the educated English did not generally believe in witchcraft. James, however, was a deeply superstitious man. He not only believed in witchcraft, but it had become an obsession which culminated with the publication of his book *Demonologie* in 1597. When he succeeded to the throne of England, he was alarmed at the general laxity on the subject, and he republished his book to ensure his new subjects realised their error. Not surprisingly, this led some to try and improve their own standing with the king by proving him right, and so the number of accusations of witchcraft rose in England during his reign. Shakespeare, who had mocked the idea of witches in his Elizabethan plays, now wrote Macbeth for James I.

So, if Lancashire, the home of so many Catholics, became the county that found, convicted and hanged more witches than any other, this would have pleased James. And that is the reason why we know so much about this particular trial. The original trial transcripts do not exist for such a remote County Assize, but what does exist is a book which was written and published by the clerk of the court, Thomas Potts, in London in 1613. It was unheard of for a clerk of the court to do so in English law – so what was his motive? The title of the book is an indication: it is called *The Wonderfull Discoverie of Witches in the Countie of Lancaster*. As a title it was designed to attract any 'royal expert' and ensured that the reader knew exactly which county was responsible. The book goes into great detail, a fact that would please a man like James who regarded himself a true scholar. The book even claimed that, despite the fact that these people had quite literally not two pins to rub together, they had somehow got hold of gunpowder – a very expensive commodity – and were planning to blow up the royal castle of Lancaster. Yes, Thomas Potts was stating that not only had the law-abiding citizens of Lancashire arrested, convicted and hanged more witches than any other county, but they had also foiled another 'gunpowder plot'. This would surely have pleased the king and the proof that it did lies in his visit to the county in 1617 – the last monarch and Duke of Lancaster to do so until 1851.

So, it can be surmised that powerful people in Lancashire were putting pressure on Bromley – and he did have a weakness. His uncle had been Chief Justice of England under Elizabeth I and he was from a notable legal family. However, Bromley had played a minor role in the Essex Rebellion in 1601, and this perhaps led to his judging cases on the less congenial Northern Circuit of Assizes later in his life and career. As a result, he may have been looking for a means to gain the recognition that would have allowed him to move to the more respectable southern circuits. He was certainly unhappy about the trial and Potts states that he began his final words at the end of the trial as follows:

> I would start by stressing that there is no man alive more unwilling to pronounce this woeful and heavy judgment against you. I would to God the cup had passed to someone else.'

He was certainly not happy about the case surrounding Alice Nutter, described as a respectable woman from Roughlee with five yeoman sons. It may have been acceptable to get away with convicting a group of vagabonds from Pendle on hearsay, but Bromley would need more to convict Mistress Nutter. So Nowell produced a witness, Alison's little sister Jennet Device, who was prepared to testify against her own kin. However, she was only nine years old and too young to take the oath. Again, Bromley should have had a problem with this and her evidence as a witness was, in reality, inadmissible. However, Nowell argued that, in the king's book, it said that children, due to their innocence, were good at identifying witches. As the king's judge, it is unlikely that Bromley would have wished to argue with the king on this matter. So Bromley let the evidence stand and, in doing so, set the legal precedent that allowed other children to be witnesses, which led eventually to the tragedy of the Salem Witch Trials 80 years later.

One question which has perplexed historians since these trials is why Alice Nutter did not defend herself. From the number of words which Thomas Potts dedicated to Alice's case, it seems that many questioned whether she was truly a witch. One possibility for her silence is that she martyred herself. Alice may have acted as a benefactor to Alison's family by supplying them with a Catholic priest. Hence, the real reason for the meeting at Malkin Tower on that day may have been religious. James, in his confession, said that the meeting was to witness a 'blessing' of Alison and adult baptism was not unknown among Catholics at the time in the Pendle Hill area. Alice may have felt it better that she, an elderly woman, hang for witchcraft, rather than be forced to reveal the presence of a priest. If caught the priest would face a traitor's death and Alice may have been influenced by the memory of her brother-in-law – Robert Nutter (not to be identified with the man of the same name said to have been bewitched by Ann Whittle and Ann Redfearn during their trial). Robert was a priest and had been persecuted and found guilty of high treason 12 years previously. He had been executed by being hung, drawn and quartered. Whilst Alice's Catholicism cannot be proven, the possibility is interesting.

Alongside the Pendle group, eight women from Samlesbury were also brought to trial for witchcraft. Ultimately, only three were tried, and the witness against them was a 14-year-old girl called Grace Sowerbutts; in this case, her age made her legally an adult. She informed the court of the horrors these women had committed on her through witchcraft. However, on this occasion, Bromley took a stronger stand than he had for the group from Pendle. He put pressure on Grace until she broke and confessed that she had been put up to it. The women had been framed because they had converted to Protestantism, whilst most members of their family had remained staunchly Catholic. A Catholic priest had been recruited to prime Grace, but he did so with more lurid continental stories of witchcraft than were known in England and this had made Bromley suspicious. The case against them was dismissed and the magistrate who had unwittingly been used to commit them for trial, Nicholas Bannister, would die later the same year.

Also on trial was Margaret Pearson of Padiham. This was her third appearance on a charge of witchcraft, and she was described by Potts as being one of the worst on trial. Even though convicted, Bromley did not sentence her to death as he had done for the Pendle group; instead she was sentenced to the stocks. Perhaps, after the conviction of the Pendle witches, Bromley felt he could show more justice to others. His discomfort on the conviction of the Pendle witches was evident when he offered them his own personal priest to attend to them before their deaths. At one point, though, he did make the remarkable statement that he hoped that they were grateful to the prosecution for taking such pains and effort to find them guilty.

However, Bromley did not show any support for the last witch on trial. This was Isobel Roby from Windle near St Helens. She was brought to trial by the aged Nicholas Bannister and was guilty it seems of not being liked by her neighbours, particularly by a Peter Chadwick. No evidence of any wrongdoing was supplied, according to Potts, simply the accusation of being a witch and this got her convicted and hanged alongside the Pendle witches. Potts does not comment on this lack of evidence and it is hard to see why Bromley, who had demanded some proper evidence even for the Pendle group, should ignore the lack of evidence in the case of Isobel. One suspects more politics behind the scenes in the case against her that has since been lost to us.

The next day, 20 August, the condemned were led up to Golgotha Hill and hanged. One of the Pendle group was not included: Alice Gray was found not guilty, though why she and not her friend Katherine was declared innocent is not explained. Ultimately, nine witches from Pendle, plus Isobel Roby, were hanged and this represents the largest single execution for witchcraft in recorded English history. Bromley was soon moved to a southern circuit and the king rewarded Potts by making him Keeper of the Public Sewers. However, the last word in this tragedy should go to that 17-year-old beggar girl, Alison. She was the last from Pendle to be brought into the court. She stood there alone and pleaded guilty, unlike the rest of them. They then brought in John Law to confront her. He was still very ill and she was taken aback at the sight of him. Before they could stop her, she climbed from the dock, and fell distraught and in tears before him. She begged him to forgive her and he did. The court was stunned. Thomas Potts goes into the details of this incident at great length in his book. However, it would not save Alison as from the moment she pleaded guilty she was doomed. But Bromley called down to her that if she was truly repentant why could she not undo her curse? Her reply brings the humanity back into this distant tragic case. To put it into a modern idiom, she replied: 'I cannot, but if my grandmother was still alive, she could have helped, she could do anything my grandmother'. As the youngest and smallest of the group, Alison would have likely taken the longest to die by the noose.

This was not the first time witches had been brought to trial at Lancaster from the Pendle area. In 1597, Roger Nowell had helped his nephew, Nicholas Starkie, bring a man named Edmund Hartley to trial for witchcraft.

Nicholas Starkie was a highly respected member of East Lancashire's Anglican community, and would later become high sheriff of the county. He was also a devoted father, and when his children fell ill with fits he had doctors brought at great expense, but to no avail. Desperate, he turned to the Catholic Church, despite his own Anglican beliefs, as he was convinced that his children had become possessed by demons, and asked a priest to perform an exorcism. The priest refused, and so he turned to a travelling magician, Edmund Hartley, for help. Edmund, through the use of charms and herbs, was able to calm the children, and as a reward Nicholas offered him 40 shillings a year. However, Edmund wanted more – namely, land and a house. This did not endear him to Nicholas, and when his children began having fits again, and the illness spread to his servants, Nicholas began to wonder if Edmund was part of the problem. So, he consulted John Dee, Elizabeth I's personal astronomer, who was at Collegiate College in Manchester. John Dee did not want to become involved, but took the time to admonish Edmund Hartley. Mr Hartley did not take the warning, and even began subjecting Nicholas' female servants to his unwanted amorous attentions. This proved his undoing. After kissing them he pursued one servant to her home, from which she had to be rescued. She claimed that when Edmund kissed her, he had breathed the devil into her. If this was her idea of revenge it worked. Edmund was arrested and taken to Lancaster Castle to be tried at the next Assizes; he was found guilty of witchcraft and sentenced to be hanged. At his execution the rope broke. Undeterred, they strung him up again and Edmund had the dubious reputation of being hanged twice for his crime. Today it seems certain that his crime was less to do with witchcraft, and more to do with taking too many liberties with his employer's generosity, and his female servants.

Neither was 1612 the end of the story of witchcraft from Pendle. Another trial involving people from the area took place 21 years later, in 1633, and this would become the sensation of its day, even more so than the trial of 1612.

The case began with a report by a young boy, Edmund Robinson, who, on returning home late, explained his lateness with a fantastic story. He said that on the way home he had met two greyhounds which had then turned into human beings. One he recognised as his neighbour's wife, Frances Dickinson. The other greyhound turned into a boy, whom Mrs Dickinson then turned into a horse and rode away to a witches' sabbat, taking Edmund with her. He was readily believed, and under encouragement from his father, went from church to church to seek those who attended that sabbat. He would point out the witches, but then say he was not sure, and in some cases change his mind. Not surprisingly, people became suspicious, particularly as his father suddenly seemed to be doing very well for himself. He was able buy cows, having previously lacked the means to do so. It was also noted that Edmund's father had two 'minders' to keep people away from asking his boy awkward questions. Soon others, taking advantage of the hysteria that had been created, decided to make their own accusations. Nicholas Cunliffe accused his neighbour, Mary Spencer, with whom he was in dispute, of witchcraft, stating that she caused a pail of water to come to her from the well. One woman from Padiham, Margaret Johnson, also stepped forward to claim that she, too, was a witch, and was happy to give a full and detailed account of witchcraft in Padiham area. For a while she gained the dubious spotlight of notoriety.

It is reported that as many as 60 men and women were accused, but only just under a third were eventually brought to Lancaster for trial – one of whom one was 'Jennet Davies'. It is likely that this was the same Jennet Device who had been the child star witness in the trial of 1612. This is not definite, but it would be ironic if it was her, especially as it was a child that now accused her.

At the trial the judge was not convinced by the evidence, and dismissed all but seven of the defendants, who were then imprisoned. Of these, three would die in prison, with the remaining four being Mary Spencer, Margaret Johnson, Frances Dickinson and Jennet Hargreaves.

The news of this major discovery of witches in Lancashire caused a sensation when it reached London. The playwrights Thomas Heywood and Richard Browne wrote and produced a play to cash in on the sensation, entitled *The Late Lancashire Witches*. The case also came to the attention of the king, Charles I (1625–49), who wanted to know more. He first ordered the four surviving convicted witches to be brought to London for further investigation. Frances Dickinson and Mary Spencer both revealed that they were victims of disputes with their accusers. Frances also informed Charles' investigators that Edmund's father had told her husband that for 40 shillings he could have his wife freed. As a result, the king decided to have Edmund brought to London. Free from the influence of his father and his chaperones, the boy confessed that he had made it all up to avoid a beating from his father for being late. History is not sure whether all the suspected witches were subsequently released, or if some of them continued to languish in Lancaster Castle until they died. This has certainly been suggested as the fate of Jennet Device, who is said to have still been in the castle in 1636.

The last word must go to Heywood and Browne, who added to the end of the play the following lines,

> ... Perhaps great mercy
> After just condemnation, give them a day
> Of longer life...

> One hopes they did have a longer life.

The year 1666 saw the last-known person executed for witchcraft at the Lancaster Assizes, Isobel Rigby from Wigan.

The English Civil War and the Jacobites

The people of Lancashire were divided in their loyalties during the English Civil War (1642–51), but this was not uncommon as communities and families nationally were torn between king and parliament. Manchester, Bolton and Rochdale were staunchly parliamentarian, whilst, from the outset, Preston, Warrington and Wigan were for the king.

As Lancaster possessed a castle owned by the Duke of Lancaster, King Charles I, it might be expected that its citizens would be royalist, but in actual fact their attitude can best be described as ambivalent. Religion played a crucial role with non-conformists siding almost universally with the parliamentarians against those faithful to the Church of England who supported the king. As mentioned previously, Lancashire had remained a 'hotbed' of Catholicism following the Reformation. The county was a long way from London and the king's court, the terrain was wild and it was very difficult for the authorities to impose their will and maintain law and order. Despite the fact that Catholics had suffered a prolonged period of persecution for their supposed disloyalty to the crown, their loyalties were almost exclusively in favour of the king. Unfortunately, due to the continued suspicions surrounding them, Catholics were not allowed to carry weapons and, as a result, the forces loyal to the king in Lancashire were deprived of an important source of manpower during the initial stages of the conflict.

The first months of the war did not go well for the Lancashire royalists and Preston fell to parliamentarian forces fairly quickly.

Having secured this important town, a force was then sent north to discover how well Lancaster was fortified and garrisoned. Probably to his great surprise, the commander, Sergeant Major Birch, discovered that he was able to enter Lancaster without difficulty and found the citizens more than willing to accept his presence. He was probably even more shocked when, on his approach to the castle, the royalist forces commanded by Sir John Girlington ran away and abandoned it to him. Thus, Birch was able to take both the town and castle with barely a shot being fired. As was usual in such circumstances, the victorious parliamentarians subsequently freed all the prisoners they found in the castle – in truth, they probably did not want the hassle of looking after them. We can only imagine how the king felt when he learned how easily Lancaster and his castle had fallen to the enemy. It was particularly embarrassing as Charles was the Duke of Lancaster and therefore parliament would have been able to capitalise on the great symbolic significance of gaining this prize. To be fair, Girlington was probably unprepared to withstand any kind of siege, but the fact that he put up no resistance at all undoubtedly damaged the royalist image, at least locally.

The royalists could not allow this state of affairs to stand and, shortly afterwards, the Earl of Derby, the royalist commander in Lancashire, led a force from the south of the county to retake the town and the castle. If he moved quickly, he would have been able to attack before the parliamentarians could be reinforced and their position strengthened. He knew that only a small force of about 600 men occupied Lancaster and that they lacked artillery and ammunition. Unfortunately for the earl, something happened which forced him to change his plans: a Spanish ship named the *Santa Anna* was shipwrecked at the mouth of the river Wyre. It would have been disastrous for him if the parliamentarians were able to get their hands on the 20 cannon she carried before he did. The race was on, and a force of parliamentarians set out from Preston, whilst the Earl of Derby rushed to the spot with a detachment of his own men. Although Derby arrived first, he could not actually carry the cannon away. As a result, he burned the ship, hoping to make the cannon inaccessible, and then left. But his plan was unsuccessful – the cannon were salvaged by his adversaries and taken to Lancaster.

Undeterred, the Earl of Derby continued on his march to Lancaster with 3,000–4,000 troops and attacked the town on the morning of 18 March 1643, catching the parliamentarians completely by surprise. Refusing to surrender, the parliamentarians put up a stern resistance and successfully repelled the first royalist attack. Derby, however, rallied his men and led a second attack which overwhelmed his opponents, who retreated to the safety of the castle. Most made it, but some were not so lucky – Captain William Shuttleworth MP was killed just outside the gatehouse whilst fighting a rearguard action, along with a large number of men from the town. The bullet holes can still be seen on the gatehouse, acting as a permanent reminder of this action. During this attack, many buildings in the town were set on fire by Derby's troops – the fires subsequently spread, causing considerable damage to homes and businesses. They also looted the town and killed a number of civilians – parliamentarian sources later claimed that the royalists barbarously cut the throats of their victims (men, women and children) with butchers' knives. Others, including the mayor, were taken prisoner. Yet, overall, the attack was a failure – the Earl of Derby did not succeed in retaking the castle or the town and the associated damage and casualties only served to harm the royalist cause further. Fearing a parliamentarian relief force arriving from Preston, the royalists were forced to evacuate Lancaster on 19 March and retreat southwards, setting fire to many buildings before they left. Derby did have some luck, however; the parliamentarian force moving north against him had left Preston with an insufficient garrison. Derby bypassed this force and fell on Preston, recapturing it for the king. In 1645, Lancaster was awarded £8000 from the captured estates of royalist supporters to help rebuild those areas damaged during this attack.

In June 1643, there was another short-lived attempt by forces loyal to the king to take Lancaster, led by Sir John Girlington from Hornby Castle. He held Lancaster Castle under siege for 20 days until the arrival of a substantial parliamentarian force forced his retreat.

At the conclusion of the first civil war in 1646, a garrison was placed at the castle which consisted of a 'rude company of Yorkshire troopers', who stabled their horses in the keep. In 1648, during the second civil war, Thomas Tyldesley besieged the castle for a short time, but was forced to retreat north following the royalist defeat at the Battle of Preston. A year later, parliament ordered that the walls of the castle were to be demolished as part of a general demilitarisation of castles throughout the country. At first there was some resistance to the order which came from parliament – the building was, after all, the county gaol. Interestingly, it was at this time that large numbers of anti-government rioters from various towns in Lancashire were imprisoned at the castle. Parliament was insistent, however, and so the authorities gave in and much of the medieval castle was demolished. Buildings on the west and south sides were retained which allowed for the court to function and provided accommodation for prisoners, but, from 1649 until 1667, Lancaster Castle was effectively a gaol without any walls.

On 12 August 1651, Lancaster Castle had a brief brush with royalty once again when Charles II passed through the town whilst heading south in an attempt to reclaim his crown following the execution of his father, Charles I, in 1649. Charles was proclaimed king to the town's inhabitants in Market Square and he ordered all of the prisoners to be released from the castle. On this occasion he was defeated at the Battle of Worcester later in the same year and the castle had to wait until his restoration in 1660 before some effort was made to repair the damage inflicted by parliament. By this time the castle was in an almost ruinous state, with, in addition to the demolished walls, repair work required to the rooves, towers, gatehouse and lodgings. In 1663 a group of commissioners were appointed to commission and oversee the rebuilding of the walls and the other repair work – the estimated cost was £1957. This work was undertaken in 1667, but not all of the required repairs were completed; for example, only half of the keep was re-roofed, with the other half left unroofed and unused. The new walls were not as high or as thick as those which had preceded them. Furthermore, the full circuit of walls was also not completed at this time; a 1778 plan of the castle clearly shows that even by that date there was no wall between the Gatehouse and Well Tower.

The Jacobite Rebellions

On 7 November 1715, a Jacobite army entered Lancaster and proclaimed the 'Old Pretender', James Francis Edward Stuart, as King James III in Market Square to a largely hostile populace. After (again) setting all the prisoners free from the castle, the army left the town on 9 November and was subsequently defeated at the Battle of Preston (9–14 November 1715). Following this defeat hundreds of Jacobite rebels were imprisoned in the castle and such were their numbers that the stables had to be employed to keep them in; a regiment of dragoons was billeted in Lancaster to guard them. The king granted the prisoners 2d. per day for bread, 1d. for cheese and 1d. for beer. Some were later sent to Liverpool to stand trial, whilst the remainder were tried at Lancaster Castle. Nine are known to have been hanged and their heads (with name-labels attached) were fixed on the gatehouse. At least 47 died of natural causes whilst in prison, and many more were tried and subsequently sent as convicts to the American colonies.

Thirty years later, on 24 November 1745, the 'Old Pretender's' son, Charles Edward Stuart ('Bonnie Prince Charlie') entered Lancaster at the head of his army. He was proclaimed regent on behalf of his father in Market Square and a plaque near the site now commemorates this. Charles stayed the night at a house on Church Street but departed the following day – he would return to Lancaster in full retreat on 13 December. Again, many of his followers were captured during the retreat and imprisoned at the castle. On this occasion, however, they were not tried or punished at Lancaster – most were conveyed to Carlisle for that purpose.

Plaque commemorating Bonnie Price Charlie's visit to Lancaster in 1745. Photograph by Colin Penny

Debtors

A DEBTOR IS SOMEONE WHO OWES MONEY to another person, known as the creditor. The first Debtors' Act was passed by King Edward III in 1351. The idea behind the new law was to boost the economy by making lending more attractive, since those willing to lend money would now have a means of justice should the loan not be repaid. The Act stipulated that debtors who did not repay their debt could be imprisoned until such a time as the outstanding amount was settled. The Act did not state a minimum amount, so in theory a debtor could be imprisoned for owing as little as a penny. This opened the door to malicious and ridiculous law suits, and many people found themselves in prison for owing very small amounts of money. Over time, debtors became the largest proportion of inmates within most county gaols and were a significant burden on the system and a major cause of prison overcrowding. In London the problem was so great that by the eighteenth century two huge prisons were used to accommodate debtors – the Fleet and the Marshalsea. Frequently, debtors were forced to remain in prison for one week for every shilling they owed.

During the eighteenth and nineteenth centuries, attempts were made to limit the number of debtors in prison, for example by making it unattractive for creditors to incarcerate them. Once a debtor had been sent to the debtors' prison, it was no longer possible for their creditor to charge further interest on the loan or to seize their property. Moreover, there were considerable costs associated with getting the debtor to the prison. These included the court costs and also the charges made for conveying the debtor to the prison (one shilling per mile). The latter represented a very lucrative business for the court officers, especially if they conveyed more than one debtor at a time. Also, if a debtor had more than one creditor who had petitioned the court, then each one was charged the one shilling per mile regardless of the fact that it was the same person being conveyed. This worked against the drive to reduce numbers by creating a great financial incentive among some court officers to encourage as many people as possible to be sent to debtors' prison.

So, why would a creditor send someone to the debtors' prison in the first place? If they were unable to pay on the outside, it was unlikely that they would be able to pay once in prison. Not only that, but, in many instances, their family accompanied them to the prison as well. If they did not, they would become a burden on the taxpayer and this was viewed by many as completely unacceptable. A very good example of this situation was Charles Dickens, whose father was sent to the Marshalsea for debt – the whole family went too and this was why Dickens was able to write in such an informed way about life within the prison in his novel, *Little Dorritt*.

Nevertheless, from a creditor's point of view, there were still advantages to the system, apart from the merely punitive. There was, of course, a difference between people who could not pay and people who would not pay, and a spell in the debtors' prison may have convinced some of the latter to hand over their money. In addition, once in the debtors' prison, those who were considered 'worthy' candidates – for example, people who had lost money on a business venture, as opposed to those who had squandered their wealth on drink or gambling – could apply to various charitable institutions set up to help debtors. Some wealthy businessmen also occasionally left money in their wills to help debtors pay off their debt. The creditor might also be helped in recollection by the general fear of prison and the reportedly high death-rate within such institutions. This acted as a strong incentive to friends and relatives on the outside to club together and help pay off their loved one's debt – particularly if children were also imprisoned. Regarding food, poor debtors were provided with a county allowance, which in 1812 comprised bread to the value of 1*d*., and 10lbs of potatoes per week, but this was generally insufficient, particularly if they had dependants with them. This sometimes led to death and, in the late eighteenth century, around three debtors a month were starving to death in English debtors' prisons. Once a debtor was released, they then had to find their own way home, which could prove to be many miles away. It was at this time that George III introduced the minimum amount of 40s. (£2.00) for which a debtor could be sent to prison.

Most debtors' prisons were divided between the 'Masters'' side and the 'Common' side. The former was reserved for debtors who had access to money (either their own or from someone looking after them). These people could afford to pay for little luxuries, such as a cell to themselves or additional food to be brought in from outside the prison. It was also common for barbers, tailors and other tradesmen to set up shop in these establishments to serve the needs of the wealthier debtors. At Lancaster Castle traders regularly set up market stalls in the courtyard, which only served to add to the general chaos of the prison. The block now known as B-Wing was the Masters' side; this was built between 1794 and 1796, and could hold up to 500 people. In 1812 it was said to contain eight rooms, six of which measured 14' x 12'3", with the other two 19'9" x 12'3" each. These were situated above an open arcade; behind the arcade were five much smaller cells which are probably to be identified with those today known as the 'Old Cells' constructed prior to 1784. In 1812, three of the latter were being used to imprison debtors who had misbehaved; the other two were too damp to put anyone in.

Debtors paid a rent for their cell, and the cost rose with the quality of the accommodation, from 5 to 25 shillings; this was charged on entering the prison and was a one-off regardless of the length of stay. Room names included The Tap, The Snug, The Smugglers, The Pigeons, The Belle Vue, The Pin Room and The Quaker Room, as well as others that were simply numbered one to eight. Such was the Masters' side's reputation for excellent living conditions that, in the mid-nineteenth century, letters would frequently arrive addressed simply as 'Hansbrow's Hotel,

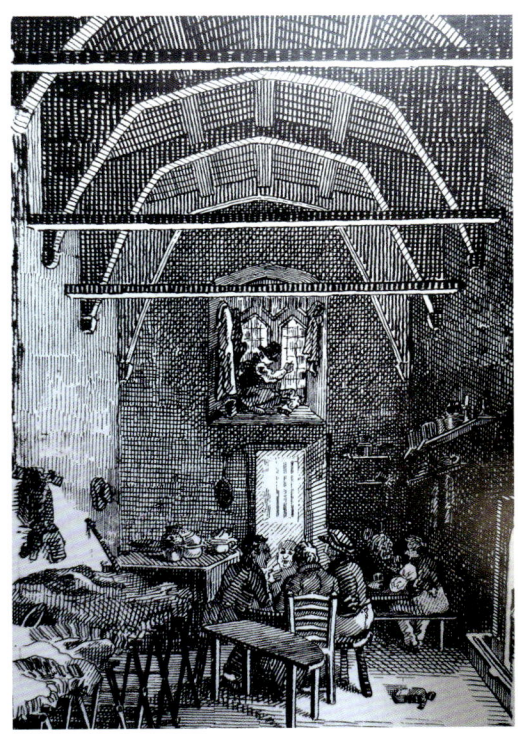

Artist's impression of some of the rooms at the debtor's prison. Clockwise from top left: 'The Snug' (Well Tower), 'The Smugglers' (Gatehouse) and The Royal Chamber (Tap) (Well Tower). Engravings by Thomas Physick, after drawings by Edward Slack. Reproduced kind permission of Lancashire County Council Museum Service

91

Watercolour by Robert Freebairn showing the Debtors' Wing shortly after its construction. Reproduced by kind permission of Lancaster City Museum

Hansbrow's Hotel, Lancaster. Photograph by Colin Penny. Used by kind permission of the Duchy of Lancaster

Lancaster'. James Hansbrow was the governor of the gaol between 1833 and 1862 and the postman knew exactly where to deliver them.

The 'Common' side was a completely different story. Here the inmates had no money and were entirely dependent upon the county allowance, the goodwill of their creditors or anyone else who took pity on them. Some were fortunate and gained employment with the debtors living on the Masters' side, serving them as butlers or cleaners. At Lancaster Castle these were known as Yardsmen and wore a special apron with a picture of the castle on it. The not-so-fortunate were often half-starved, dirty and walked around in rags. Prison reports frequently made reference to the appalling conditions. Overcrowding was endemic, with some debtors sleeping three or four to a bed, some either too ill or too dejected to get up during the day. Many of the beds, and much of the bedding was provided by charitable donation, but it was noted in 1812 that much of it in use was nearly worn out. There were no kitchens in which to prepare any food they had access to, such as the county allowance, and cooking was done in the rooms causing them to become very smoky. Such was the desperation of some individuals that they were forced to prostitute their own wives or daughters to those on the Masters' side simply to provide money to prevent starvation. At Lancaster Castle, the 'Common' debtors were frequently housed in the gatehouse.

Between 1819 and 1839, the number of debtors in Lancaster Castle rose from 193 to 320, and, in the county generally, the phrase 'gone to Lancaster' came to signify that a person was in debt. This increase can be seen in the light of growing industrialisation within the county. The number of businesses and entrepreneurial enterprises increased – but not all of these proved successful. Debtors who had some kind of trade were better placed to survive. At Lancaster Castle, a group of workshops was constructed adjacent

The Debtors' Workshops. Photograph by Colin Penny. Used by kind permission of the Duchy of Lancaster

Sketches of debtors by Edward Slack with a pencil note referring to 'Rawlinson, a blind attorney'. Reproduced by kind permission of Lancashire County Council Museum Service

to the south of the keep in which debtors could make goods to sell on the outside to help pay off their debt.

Within the prison, debtors were notoriously difficult to control. There are many recorded instances of them causing disturbances, smuggling contraband into the prison, being insubordinate, drunk and contravening prison regulations. The problem which the governors and staff faced was that these people were not criminals and were not in prison to be punished – they were simply being held until their debt was discharged. As a result, they were exempt from most forms of regulation, such as wearing a uniform, and restrictions on visitors and letters. Many were also relatively well-educated, being failed businessmen, and some were even solicitors who were well aware of the limits of official power over them and were only too willing to advise their fellow inmates. As a result, for

Hustings for the 'John O'Gaunt Borough' were held at the water pump in the castle yard. Photograph by Colin Penny. Used by kind permission of the Duchy of Lancaster

the most part, debtors were, quite literally, a law unto themselves. They had their own committees, rules and regulations, they held 'trials' for those who had infringed these rules and imposed fines on those whom they found guilty. Punishments also included being imprisoned in Hadrian's Tower for 24 hours for disturbing the peace, or a dunking in the pump for preaching temperance.

Prior to the remodelling of the prison in the 1790s, images of the courtyard clearly show a bowling green for use by the debtors and many kept themselves amused by singing, playing instruments, reading books and newspapers (there was a library which cost £1 per year to join), drinking (beer was allowed, but spirits were not) or annoying the gaolers. Some ran unofficial businesses selling beer brought in from the outside for double the cost and the poor tended to exchange their beer allowance for food, which led to even more drunkenness among the wealthier debtors. The debtors also held mock elections to amuse themselves. Hustings for the 'John O'Gaunt Borough' were held at the pump and candidates' speeches were applauded for the number of puns they contained. In 1842, the Tories beat the Liberals by 42 votes. Being elected was clearly prized as electoral bribery was rife. These elections were invariably accompanied by chaos and a great deal of drinking. Each debtor contributed, if they could, to a huge feast at the end of the proceedings. Not surprisingly, the prison surgeons frequently reported that illnesses associated with drunkenness were common among debtors. Some debtors even refused to leave when they could; the 1836 Prison Report mentions one, aged 75, who had been in the debtors' prison for 20 years and who would not leave. The 1843 Report noted a rise in the amount of illegal alcoholic spirits being smuggled into the debtors' prison and that the rooms were invariably filthy.

In 1836, the average amount of debt per debtor imprisoned in Lancaster Castle was £3. Interestingly, the costs associated with committing them to the debtors' prison averaged £3 7s.

This state of affairs could not continue indefinitely and, in the mid-nineteenth century, there was growing pressure to end the system of sending people to prison for private debt. A number of acts were passed at this time, culminating in the 1869 Bankruptcy Act, which effectively rendered debtors' prisons redundant. At Lancaster Castle, during the later nineteenth century, the former Debtors' Wing was incorporated into the felons' prison and became known as the B-Wing.

Notable Trials, Cases and Prisoners, 1795–1981

The first trial and execution of note following the opening of the new Crown Court in 1795 must be that of Dr James Case for forgery in April 1799, who tried to cheat the hangman. In the case of hanging, one could survive if the rope broke three times, the trap door stuck three times, or a combination of either of these things three times. Three being the number of the Trinity, this was seen as a sign from God that the condemned should be allowed to live. By its very nature this was difficult to engineer and proved to be an extremely rare occurrence. Another way to escape death was to actually survive the hanging – for one hour. If, when the hangman cut them down, the condemned were still alive, they were allowed to go free. After all, the sentence had been carried out – they had been executed and survived. This did happen now and then, so Case tried to engineer his survival by putting a clay pipe down his throat. Unfortunately for him, he should have used a better-quality clay pipe – it broke and he perished. His execution was the last to be held on Golgotha Hill.

It was common for the condemned to be allowed to speak from the scaffold before they met their death, as it was their last moment to seek forgiveness before they met their maker. Mary Charnley, aged only 19, who was convicted of robbery in 1808, gave a very heartfelt speech stating how sorry she was. Mary's final words were these:

> I sincerely hope my fate may be a warning to others, Farewell good people, I beg you to join in prayer with me, and assist in singing the praise of God.

So moving was her speech that the crowd watched her execution in respectful silence.

James Ogilvie said much the same at his execution in 1804:

> Before I close my eyes in eternity I will only add, that if I could foresee that the example which I set will have a salutary effect, the pains of death would be alleviated in the greatest degree.

The early nineteenth century saw a considerable increase in social and political tensions across Britain, but particularly in Lancashire. This was due to a number of factors, including the rise of the factory system, declining wages, increasing food prices and lower standards of living. Many previously prosperous families were suffering from near starvation. In the textile industry, factories could produce good quality cloth at a fraction of the cost of handloom weavers. Factory cloth could also be made by semi-skilled workers, often children, whose wages were poor compared to those of skilled home-based weavers. Not surprisingly, factories bore the brunt of popular outrage, as they were correctly seen to be the root cause of much of the economic hardship people were experiencing.

The working class also began to agitate forcefully for a greater say in the political future of the country. The beginnings of unionism can be dated to this period, as workers sought to band together to gain fair wages and better working conditions. Those in positions of authority had heard of the 'Terror' that accompanied the French Revolution and there was a real fear that the same would happen in Britain. Unions were perceived as a threat to the social and political order, and workers wanting to band together were suspected of actually wanting to overthrow the establishment. By 1812, Britain was also at war with the United States and France, whose governments had both arisen out of revolution. Internal dissent was cracked down on much more harshly than might have been the case in peacetime. There was no organised police force at this time, which meant that the military tended to deal with such disturbances, with disastrous and sometimes lethal consequences for the protestors.

On 24 April 1812, up to 100 people marched on Westhoughton and attacked the mill of Rowe and Duncough. Although many workers deserted the mob before even reaching the mill, the rioters still succeeded in setting it on fire and destroyed 180 power looms. There were also separate attacks on mills in Stockport and Middleton. Following the restoration of order, many arrests were made, with a significant number of alleged rioters committed for trial at Lancaster Castle. Unusually, a special session of the Assizes sat in May and June 1812 solely to hear cases against these defendants. The presiding judges were Sir Alexander Thomson and Sir Simon le Blanc. At the trials, it became clear that spies and *agents provocateurs* had been employed by the authorities to attend meetings prior to the outbreak of violence. They made notes of the names of those in attendance, or took descriptions, and some of them were even said to have actively encouraged the rioters in their scheme. Some went so far as to organise meetings, drawing in others who might not otherwise have taken part. They were said to have harangued the crowd, sometimes numbering around a thousand people, and whipped them up into a political frenzy. Those who tried to leave, it was said, were threatened with violence by these very same spies. Some were even accused of promising to supply a quantity of weapons. Witnesses said that the number of spies at a meeting often amounted to 25 per cent of the total, although this was almost certainly an exaggeration.

Whilst this may be an exaggeration, it is certain that spies were employed, and some probably went far beyond their remit in order to obtain the 'evidence' they believed their employers wanted. To a large degree the evidence brought against the accused was merely hearsay and unsupported accusations, which would not hold up to scrutiny in a modern trial. Some of the accused were offered their freedom in exchange for informing and giving evidence against others. Faced with the choice of co-operate or hang, it is perhaps understandable that many chose the former. As mentioned, fear of revolution was a strong incentive for harsh punishment. Although there is no evidence whatsoever that the mob had anything but the destruction of the mills and their machines in mind, it was relatively easy to paint them as revolutionaries.

Of those arrested, John Knight and 37 other men were tried at Lancaster Castle for 'administering false oaths to weavers pledging them to destroy steam looms'. They were also accused of attending a seditious meeting. Perhaps surprisingly, they were all found not guilty, but Job Fletcher, Thomas Kerfoot, James Smith and Abraham Charleson were found guilty of setting the fire that destroyed the mill and all were sentenced to death and hanged. Hannah Smith, John Howarth, John Lee and Thomas Hoyle were also hanged for stealing food during the disturbances. Of the executed, Abraham Charlson is the youngest person known to have been hanged at Lancaster Castle. According to the official records, he was 16, although his family are said to have insisted that he was only 12. Even if this had been true, it may not have saved him – the law at that time said that people as young as 11 could be hanged if capitally convicted. Abraham is said to have called out for his mother when on the gallows in the hope that she could save him. All eight were executed on 13 June 1812. Of the remainder who were tried, ten were transported for life, two were transported for seven years and thirty were imprisoned for varying terms. Amongst those transported was Thomas Holden, a weaver, who received seven years for administering a false oath.

In March 1815, George Lyon, the man reputed to be England's last great highwayman, was hanged. In reality he was a very successful 'footpad' and housebreaker, but he enjoyed the idea of being a great highwayman. He also had a romantic reputation as a womaniser, and, if half the stories are to be believed, much of the population of his home village of Upholland could be unwittingly descended from him. George's fears of dissection, a further 'punishment' for some convicted felons, were well represented in his letters which were smuggled out of the castle, via the George and Dragon Pub on the quay, to his friends and family. To prevent this happening, his friends paid the hangman to release his body to the village publican at midnight so that he could be taken by cart back to Upholland. As the publican set off from the castle, a mighty thunderstorm began and, as he described later, he felt as if the devil himself was accompanying them. On reaching home in the small hours of the morning, he was met by a torchlight parade of the villagers who had waited up to greet their local hero. George was 54 years old when he was executed and was buried in his mother's grave in the local churchyard.

In 1817, four men – William Holden and three members of the Ashcroft family – were condemned for the brutal murder of two household servants during a housebreaking in Pendleton, near Salford. They declared their innocence in court, as was common in many cases, but they also continued to do so whilst on scaffold. As one declared, whilst the noose was put about his neck, 'I declare we are innocent, and I would not tell a lie for all the world'. This visibly shocked the crowd. It was said that surely no one about to meet their Maker would deny his guilt unless he was innocent. As one commenter, Joseph Hall, wrote:

> After this execution, nothing could exceed the excitement which has kept alive upwards of twelve months, everyone being kept quite satisfied of the innocence of the culprits

One of the more famous political agitators of the nineteenth century to have been imprisoned at Lancaster Castle was Samuel Bamford. In 1817 Bamford was imprisoned at Salford on suspicion of high treason because of his radical politics. He was subsequently sent to London and secured his release through a promise of good behaviour, after which he returned home to Middleton, near Manchester.

On 16 August 1819, however, he attended a meeting at St Peter's Field in Manchester at which the famed radical, Henry Hunt (known to his enemies as 'The Orator'), was due to speak. But disaster ensued when the cavalry was ordered into the crowd to clear a path for constables, who were looking to arrest Hunt. Losing control of themselves, their horses and their swords, they plunged into the crowd of up to 100,000 people and hacked their way through to the stage where Hunt and the other organisers were stood. Eleven people were killed (including one constable, accidentally) and hundreds injured. The event has since become known to history as the Peterloo Massacre. The local magistrates argued that the meeting and its organisers were radicals who were intent upon the violent overthrow of the government – Bamford was recognised as attending and later arrested. On this occasion he was charged with treason and taken to The New Bailey at Salford. Later he was transferred to Lancaster Castle.

Samuel Bamford is particularly valuable to us because he is one of only a few prisoners who wrote about what conditions were like at Lancaster Castle. Although written over 20 years after his stay, his book *Passages in the Life of a Radical* provides us with what is probably the most detailed and vivid description of prison life in the nineteenth century. As a high-profile prisoner, on arrival at the castle, he was made to wait in the gatehouse until the son of the prison governor arrived. He tells us that his group was then taken to the debtors' yard where they were received by the inmates as heroes. He refers to the walls of the castle being 'high and frowning barriers of masonry', with 'moveable spikes', and describes the sense of claustrophobia as feeling like being 'trapped in a well'.

Initially, he was taken to the 'criminal ward', which contained a tower known as the 'Round Tower' – this he described as 'inconvenient, cold and comfortless', with a constant draught which caused the smoke from the chimney to blow into the room, and affected both his breathing and his eyes. He was soon moved, however, to the 'next ward but one' where he felt 'comparatively at home'. Here he and the other people arrested with him were kept together, separated from the other prisoners. The building had a day room with 'a good kettle and pan', and a water pump in the yard, and the whole area appeared clean and airy. They were able to send into Lancaster for other kitchen utensils and groceries, pending the arrival of their prison allowance. They lit a fire, made a good breakfast and were 'quite merry'. They even 'employed' another prisoner who was less comfortably off to clean their rooms in exchange for additional food supplied by them. All in all, Bamford stated that he 'imbibed a favourable opinion of this prison', with the rooms 'as white and sweet as quicklime could make them' and lit by the morning sun. The bed consisted of an iron slab full of perforations, resting on projections from the walls, a straw mattress, a couple of blankets and a good horse rug.

His good opinion, however, was not to last. On the second night in his cell he became subject to terrible bouts of coughing and could not breathe – he said he felt like he was 'closed up in a coffin'. The only way he could get any relief was by kneeling up in bed and trying to breathe in the draught that came from the ventilation hole above the cell door. Henry Hunt, who had also been sent to Lancaster, was bailed the following day, but moving to Hunt's old cell did not help. Bamford noted that the prison doctor gave him a mixture that helped a little, but he still found it impossible to lie down for most of the nights he was incarcerated. Bamford recorded other attempts to keep the prison population healthy, including mandatory examinations for skin disease.

With regard to the prison diet, he stated that the allowance consisted of gruel, bread, potatoes, soup and butcher's meat. A small amount of butter was also given twice a week, but half of this was later changed to cheese. In order to keep their spirits up, the prisoners entertained themselves by chatting, singing, telling stories, playing hopping and leaping matches, walking in the yard, writing letters, reading letters (in small doses) and reading newspapers. They also attended the prison chapel on prayer days and Sundays, and sang the 'Lancashire Hymn' every night before locking up time.

On the day of his hearing, Bamford tells us that he was walked through the round tower, through another yard, through a part of the Great Tower, and into a long room at the back known as the Sweating Room – so called because it was here that people waited before being taken into court. When it was his turn, he was led down some steps, along a subterranean passage, and then climbed some steps into the dock, which was surmounted by iron spikes. The courtroom was crowded and lit by lamps and chandeliers. He referred to it as a place 'to inspire awe and alarm'. He was accompanied in the dock by several prison officers, with the deputy governor in a small space to one side. Javelin men took up position behind the dock. On the bench was the judge, Baron Wood, together with the high sheriff, and the judge's friends and family. The charge was read, to which he pleaded 'not guilty', and the case was postponed to the next Assizes – Bamford was required to provide bail for £200. Having obtained this, he was released on 17 September.

In the event, he did not return to Lancaster Castle. Instead, his trial took place at the York Assizes, where he was found guilty and imprisoned at Lincoln for one year. Henry Hunt, who was imprisoned for a short time with Samuel Bamford, was also found guilty at York and served over two years in prison. Like Bamford, he advocated a non-violent approach towards political and social reform and was very influential in the rise of the Chartist movement.

Three years after the Peterloo Massacre, it seemed that justice would finally be done for those who had been killed and injured. In April 1822 four members of the Manchester Yeomanry were prosecuted for wounding Thomas Redford. This action was taken against Captain Hugh Hornby Birley, Captain Richard Withington, Trumpeter Edward Meagher and Private Alexander Oliver. The hearing lasted five days and, although many witnesses gave evidence against the accused, a ruling was given they had acted lawfully in their duty of dispersing an illegal gathering.

A continuing decline in standards of living and working conditions, together with increasing food prices and rising unemployment in Lancashire, led to further outbreaks of violence. By 1826, only 40 per cent of those who could work were in paid employment and attempts to induce parliament to introduce a tax on cloth produced by power looms as well as a minimum wage for weavers failed.

On 24 April 1826, about 1000 people assembled on Whinney Hill, near Accrington. They were armed with sledgehammers, cudgels and various other weapons. Over the course of the next few days, a large number of mills were destroyed in Accrington, Oswaldtwistle, Blackburn, Over Darwen, Garsden, Helmshore, Rawtenstall, Edenfield, Chorley and Bacup. Initially, troops on the scene did very little and some were observed to be sharing their rations. This was probably done more out of sympathy for the rioters' hunger than for any other reason, but it led some to believe that the army was on their side. This belief did not last long. At Chatterton, on 26 April, the Riot Act was read and the army opened fire on the crowd, killing six people, including two innocent bystanders. Many other people were wounded. The rioters fled and this effectively put an end to the disturbances. Nevertheless, a total of 1100 looms had been destroyed. As in 1812, arrests ensued over the following weeks, with the accused (53 men and 12 women) being tried at the Preston Quarter Sessions and Lancaster Assizes. In total, 35 men and 6 women were sentenced to death, but all were subsequently reprieved. Eight men and two women, however, were transported for life, and we know something of the life of one of them – Mary Hindle.

On 25 April, rioters attacked the mill of William Turner at Helmshore. There was no doubt that Mary was present, as a government agent in the crowd cut a piece of material from the dress she was wearing as proof of her involvement. Eyewitnesses also claimed that she actively encouraged those taking part in the disorder, laughing and shouting: 'I have won my bet, I bet a shilling that the power looms would be destroyed within five weeks'. During her trial at Lancaster Castle, Mary claimed that she was trying to retrieve her child who had run into the crowd. Popular sympathy was undoubtedly on her side and even the mill owner pleaded on her behalf. She was, however, convicted and sentenced to death, although this was later commuted to transportation for life. She arrived in Australia in 1827 and was put to work in a laundry. Four years later she was issued with a ticket of leave, which was renewed in 1835. This gave her a certain amount of freedom as long as she did not leave the town of Sydney. In 1838 she ran away, but was recaptured after three weeks. She was then sent to the Paramatta Female Factory, but again tried to escape en route. She then wrote to the governor asking for a free pardon, but this was refused. After a brief period away from Paramatta, working as a laundress, she was back by 24 August 1841 having again tried to run away. It was on that date that she took her own life in the Female Factory.

On occasions the Shire Hall has also been used for criminal cases, and one of these occurred in 1827 – the trial of Mr Edward Gibbon Wakefield and his brother, George, for abduction. Wakefield was a member of the government's diplomatic corps and wanted to advance his political career. To do so he needed to gain a seat in parliament and, at that time, with about one-third of the seats available for purchase, this was a realistic possibility with the right amount of cash. To achieve this, he used the traditional eighteenth-century method of abducting an heiress, marrying her and using the threat of scandal against her family to force them to acquiesce to the marriage. However, for Wakefield, either times had moved on or perhaps he had picked the wrong family to intimidate, for his abduction of the heiress, Ellen Turner, and their subsequent marriage led not to wealth but directly to court. As a member of society, he was afforded the dignity of being tried in the Shire Hall, rather than in the Crown Court, where common felons were dealt with, and a painting of his trial can be seen in the Drop Room. He was found guilty and served three years in the Fleet Prison in London before being accepted back into society. Later, he would emigrate and become one of the founding fathers of the New Zealand dominion and of its capital.

March 1828 saw the execution of Jane Scott, aged 21, who had lived at Marsh Lane, Preston, and who was convicted for the murder of her mother. The motive was money. On the day of her execution, she collapsed, too ill to walk or stand, so an old clerk's chair was found to which wheels were attached and in this she was

The Trial of Edward Gibbon Wakefield by Dawson Watson. Reproduced by kind permission of Lancashire County Council Museum Service

The wheeled chair used to convey Jane Scott to her execution. Photograph by Colin Penny. Used by kind permission of Lancashire County Council's Museums Service

conveyed across the castle and on to the scaffold. It was said that she looked more dead than alive when the noose was put around her neck. It was reported that her execution attracted the largest crowd ever assembled for such an event at the castle. The chair itself can still be seen today in the Drop Room. After her execution, as was allowed by the law, Jane's body was taken away for dissection for medical purposes. Later, her small skeleton was to be found behind a curtain in a Preston shop and the owner charged a small fee to lift the curtain; he would even allow children to shake its hand. The skeleton was lost sometime during the very early twentieth century.

John Diggle, who was executed in 1826 for the murder of Benjamin Cass and his wife Alice, wrote a song to perform at his execution – known as 'Diggle's Ditty'. His song ended thus:

> Spectators this ditty I wish to conclude
> Beware of sad passion and never be rude
> I am guilty of murder, says Diggles, I know
> At Lancaster Castle, I fulfilled the law

Sadly, the records do not tell us whether or not he received a round of applause.

Probably the most famous civil case to be held in the Shire Hall was also one of the longest civil cases in English legal history. This was Wright versus Tatham in the early nineteenth century. It was a dispute over a will, concerning a major land inheritance, Hornby Castle. Mr Tatham brought the case as he could not bear that his deceased cousin should have left land to Mr Wright, a mere estate steward. It took just over 13 years to settle, with Mr Tatham the winner in 1838; not surprisingly, the lawyers' fees were considerable. It would give way to the legend of court cases reducing plaintiffs to penury, and was taken up by Charles Dickens in his novel Bleak House. Mr Wright lost the case due to his inability to prove that his master was in his right mind precisely at the moment that the will granting him the estate was signed and witnessed. As a result, from then on, if a will was likely to be contested, there had to be a statement to the effect that the person making it was in their right mind at the time, and that this was witnessed. The case has remained a component for study in the modern instruction of civil law to this day, and is easily found online.

Some Chartists were also brought to trial at Lancaster Castle, and chief among them was Feargus O'Connor. The Chartists were a working-class organisation which campaigned for the adoption by parliament of 'The Charter' – a document which called for the reform of parliament and the voting system. The 1832 Reform Act had left most of the population without the right to vote and this led to widespread discontent and political agitation. The six points that the Chartists demanded were:

> Votes for all men aged 21 and over
> A secret ballot
> Annual Parliaments
> Payments for MPs
> The abolition of the property qualification for MPs
> Electoral districts of equal size

Feargus O'Connor became the acknowledged leader of the Chartist movement and his newspaper, the *Northern Star*, was its national mouthpiece. Rioting and violence erupted again in Lancashire during 1842 and these disturbances became known as the Plug

Riots, due to the actions of strikers pulling the plugs out of factory machinery to stop them working. The call was for a general strike and for all work to cease until the People's Charter had been ratified as the law of the land. Nationally, it is believed that around half a million people took part in the strikes, but whether the majority was concerned more with the adoption of the Charter, or with low wages and poor living conditions is a debatable point. Although Feargus and the other Chartist leaders had called for peaceful protest, there were many instances of violence. In Preston four people were shot during a riot on 13 August 1842 in Lune Street – a memorial now stands on the spot where they were killed. Following the restoration of order, Feargus and 58 other men were tried at Lancaster Castle for inciting riots, risings, strikes and disorder. Charges against seven were dropped and 19 were found not guilty. Feargus O'Connor was convicted, but the case was adjourned for sentencing and he was bailed. Perhaps reluctant to make a martyr of him and increase O'Connor's influence, the court was never reconvened and he was never sentenced. A number of other Chartists are known to have been sentenced to hard labour at Lancaster Castle. At their trial at the Kirkdale Quarter Sessions, they were accused of

> having assembled together in a tumultuous manner, and by loud shouts and intimidation terrified the peaceable inhabitants of Leigh, in this county, and there, and by their violent and inflammatory language endeavoured to excite the persons so assembled to cease from labour, and to hold a national holy day, and exciting them to acts of violence against the property and persons of Her Majesty's liege subjects resident in the Leigh Union.

Public hangings continued at Hanging Corner until 1868 when parliament abolished public executions altogether. The last person to be publicly hanged at Lancaster Castle was Stephen Burke in 1865, who had been convicted for the murder of his wife, whom he had beaten to death in front of their children. The noose believed to have been used for this execution remains on display in the Drop Room.

With the arrival of private executions, hangings carried out at Lancaster Castle used the more humane 'long drop' and, until 1887, the scaffold was built out from the steps to the Chapel (situated in the keep) into Chapel Yard. However, this was not high enough, so the paving stones in front of the steps were pulled up and a hole deep enough for the drop was dug under the supervision of the hangman. Rather than replace the stones, the hole was just filled up with earth, ready for the next time. In the meantime, it was used as a flowerbed and, following the last hanging there in 1887, it has remained a flowerbed. The last execution at Lancaster Castle was not carried out in Chapel Yard. Instead they used another yard behind A-Wing, known ever since as the Topping Yard, and there in November 1910 Thomas Rawcliffe of Lancaster was hanged.

Thomas Rawcliffe had turned himself in for the murder of his wife and, on his own confession, was tried for wilful murder. The police then changed their mind, with the chief constable of the county himself informing the court that they regarded his action as manslaughter because Thomas was mentally ill. The jury agreed, but as Rawcliffe insisted he had murdered his wife, they had to find him guilty and looked to the judge for mercy. The judge did not believe any of it – declaring Thomas no more than a drunkard, he sentenced him to death. Despite much protest and petitions at this decision, Rawcliffe was hanged on 15 November, the last person to be hanged at Lancaster Castle.

On 12 December 1910 death came to Lancaster Castle. Anne, the daughter and housekeeper of the Court Keeper, William Bingham, began complaining of severe stomach pains and died very suddenly. No one thought it strange, even after Mr Bingham himself suddenly died only a few weeks later. He had been the Court Keeper for 30 years and was described as a fit 70-year-old man. However, he had also been complaining of stomach cramps in the weeks leading up to his death. A writing case commissioned by him for Queen Victoria's Diamond Jubilee in 1897 is kept in the Grand Jury Room. His son Robert, aged 37, succeeded as the residential Court Keeper and took up the accommodation at the castle that came with the post. Although not lived in anymore, this area is now used as offices by Lancashire County Council. Robert's sister, Edith,

Position of the gallows, 1868–1887; the former drop is now the flower bed. Photograph by Carnegie Publishing. Used by kind permission of the Duchy of Lancaster

Thomas Rawcliffe. Reproduced by kind permission of Lancashire County Council Museum Service

who had been the cook, now took over as housekeeper. However, after six months, Robert decided to bring his half-sister Margaret in as housekeeper because he considered Edith not up to the job. On the day of Margaret's arrival, Edith prepared breakfast for her and, a few hours later, Margaret collapsed and died. Incredibly, even then, the doctors saw nothing suspicious. James reluctantly asked Edith to be the housekeeper again, but it did not work out. A month later, James told Edith he was hiring another new housekeeper. The following day, after breakfast, he set off to give a tour of the courts, but half-way through he suddenly collapsed and died. At last, the fact that so many deaths had occurred in one family in such a short period of time raised suspicion. An order was obtained to exhume the bodies and all were found to have died of severe arsenic poisoning. Edith was the cook in each case and she had been known to use a weed killer containing arsenic in the castle garden located at the rear of the building. Two empty tins were found hidden and Edith was arrested. A coroner's court had no hesitation in finding that Edith Bingham had wilfully murdered her relatives and committed her for trial. However, as there were no witnesses to her putting the poison in the food, she was acquitted on the grounds of reasonable doubt. She would die many years later in a mental hospital.

In 1975 the Shire Hall hosted one of the most sensational criminal cases of the late twentieth century, which would also prove to be one of worst miscarriages of justice in British legal history. This was the trial of the Birmingham Six – a terrorist trial which saw six Irishman convicted of carrying out the Birmingham bombings of the previous year and who were sentenced to life imprisonment. The judge at the trial said that it was shame the death penalty was no longer an option. It was just as well it wasn't as they were undoubtedly innocent. At an appeal hearing 16 years later all six were proved to be innocent and freed.

The Shire Hall would host another sensational criminal case five years later, known as the Case of the Handless Corpse. This was the trial of Terry Sinclair, a drugs kingpin from New Zealand, for the murder of his business partner, Martin Johnstone, who was known as Mr Asia. It was a bungled hit by Sinclair's henchman,

The writing case commissioned by Willliam Bingham for Queen Victoria's Diamond Jubilee in 1897, kept in the Grand Jury Room. Photograph by Colin Penny. Used courtesy of Lancashire County Council Museum Service

who had been ordered to kill Johnstone, that led to their arrests. The murder took place in Lancashire as Sinclair was operating his drug business out of Moss Side, Leyland. Sinclair was regarded as a very dangerous man; snipers were placed on the roof of the castle and armed police were positioned all around Castle Hill. The judge, jury and prosecution were kept under armed guard in safe houses throughout the trial. Sinclair did not bother with a defence counsel, and read a book through the whole trial, under the assumption the jury dare not find him guilty. They did and he died three years into his life sentence.

Today, both courts still operate, but on a far lesser scale. The Crown Court is used for comparatively low-level criminal cases and the Shire Hall hosts occasional civil cases and inquests. However, as they still operate, Lancaster Castle remains the last working royal castle in England, continuing to administer justice as it has done for over 800 years.

Prison Reform

The notion of prison as a place of punishment and long-term imprisonment is a relatively modern idea. Originally, prisons were predominantly used as places where people were kept before their trial or whilst awaiting another form of punishment – such as flogging, transportation to the colonies or execution. Punishment was a public ritual – it was supposed to be seen to be done and served as a warning and lesson to anyone who contemplated embarking on a similar path. It also provided the victims of crime with a visible retribution, and it was not uncommon for the bodies of executed criminals to be sent to the places of their crimes to be hung in chains or gibbeted to allow the community a form of closure. Generally, the only people locked up were either debtors, who comprised the majority of the imprisoned, petty offenders sentenced to a very short term of imprisonment, or vagrants. The latter two groups were not even supposed to be sent to the prisons but kept in separate houses of correction or bridewells. In reality, however, many were sent to prisons simply for the sake of convenience. The exception to the above rule were high-ranking political prisoners, such as those who had been accused of plotting against the monarch; they could sometimes be kept in prison for years (even decades) without trial and were usually confined in the Tower of London.

Increased urbanisation and industrialisation during the late eighteenth and early nineteenth centuries, together with falling wages and increased poverty, led to a massive rise in crime at this time – particularly petty crime. Matters were made worse following the loss of Britain's American colonies following the

Revolutionary War (1775–83). Suddenly, prisons had to accommodate thousands of prisoners who would have been transported and this led to dreadfully overcrowded conditions. Although transportation was resumed in 1788, this time to Australia, the crime rate continued to increase, causing the crisis of overcrowding in prisons to worsen. By 1840 the prison population nationally was three times what it had been in the late eighteenth century – standing at 13,000 inmates. In most cases prisons could no longer cope with the influx of prisoners. Overcrowding was not helped by the use of some prisons for prisoners of war; at Lancaster Castle, we know of at least one prisoner taken during the American Revolutionary War, and many more French prisoners taken during the Napoleonic Wars. Nationally, attempts were made to ease the problem through increasing the use of convict transportation, but without much success.

Prior to the nineteenth century, prisons were quite chaotic with very little attempt made to regulate or control the behaviour of the inmates. Men, women and children were kept in the same prisons and frequently shared the same cells. There were large numbers of debtors and most county gaols also doubled as the county asylum. People with mental health illnesses were placed in prison simply to get them off the streets and out of the hands of the local authorities. Prisons were wholly unsuited to care for the needs of these people and, at Lancaster Castle, the governor John Higgin Jr (1783–1833) sent a number of letters to the Home Office, advocating their removal to more suitable accommodation. He also sent his son, Thomas, to the asylum in Manchester to learn how to treat those in his care more effectively. The opening of the Lancaster Moor Hospital in 1816 should have put an end to this, but misdiagnosed prisoners, who were undoubtedly ill, were still being sent to Lancaster Castle prison in the mid-nineteenth century. The increasingly severe regimes imposed on prisoners after the 1830s also had the effect of destabilising people further. Prison populations were sometimes reduced through outbreaks of disease, such as typhoid, cholera and typhus (gaol fever), but epidemics only added to the chaotic conditions. Disease was not solely confined to the prisoners; John Higgin Sr (appointed gaoler of Lancaster

Castle in 1779) died from typhus at the age of 48 in December 1783. The Assizes are also known to have been suspended on a number of occasions due to outbreaks of disease in the castle and at least one judge is known to have perished whilst presiding in the Crown Court.

The chaos and disorder were not helped by the fact that, until 1774, gaolers were not paid a wage for doing their job. They responded by running their prisons as unofficial private enterprises, charging rents for cells and running a tavern (known as 'the Tap') to supplement their incomes – prisoners were more like customers, and rowdy ones, than inmates. An earlier gaoler at the castle, John Dane, was himself a heavy drinker who allowed his prisoners to drink and gamble freely. Two of his daughters ran the Tap, which was situated in the Well Tower, and the prison even had its own brewery. In 1779 John Dane hanged himself from a jack in the kitchen of the Judges' Lodgings because a debtor had escaped custody. In such circumstances, the gaoler was held financially accountable.

The ready availability of alcohol and the relatively low number of turnkeys (wardens) made it nearly impossible to maintain order in most prisons. The system of charging prisoners who were awaiting trial a rent for their cell also contributed to the problem of prison overcrowding. If a prisoner could not afford to pay the fees owed to the gaoler, then they could not be released, even if found not guilty at their trial. Effectively, they went from being a remand prisoner to being a debtor unable to discharge their debt, and would continue to remain in prison until the debt was paid. Thus, some unfortunate people found themselves in the terrible situation of being declared not guilty at their trial, but still remaining in prison for years, and even decades, because they were never able to pay the fees – fees which continued to rise with every additional day they remained in prison. These prisoners were neglected because they contributed nothing to the gaoler's income. The introduction of salaries for gaolers in 1774 ended this fee system – but a Tap continued to operate at many prisons, including at Lancaster Castle. In 1784 most of the gaoler's combined official and unofficial annual earnings of £360 came from the sale of alcohol. A year later he was put on an official salary, in exchange for which he was supposed to give up all unofficial income. The salary, however, was only £210 and it is most unlikely that many gaolers decided to accept such a drastic wage cut and adhered strictly to the new rules. Over time this seems to have been acknowledged by the authorities; in 1798 the salary was increased to £400, and by 1812 the gaoler's combined salary and fees (such as for the transfer convicts sentenced to transportation to ports on the south coast) came to £700 plus lodgings, and by 1840 the salary alone was £600.

By the late eighteenth century, prison reformers were arguing for an end to the disordered regime in Britain's prisons. They advocated the imposition of a new system based on regulation, hard work, religious instruction and nightly solitary confinement to bring about a reform in prisoner conduct and morals. Prison was seen as benefiting neither society nor the inmates themselves, as their character was likely to be worse on release than when they went in. This was particularly the case for petty offenders, who mixed with hardened criminals, who tended to either bully them or teach them the 'tricks of the trade'. Segregation of the sexes was also seen as key to establishing order – it was argued that men and women should be kept separate for their moral good. Prisoners should also be classified according to their type or offence, and separated accordingly to end the possibility of moral 'infection' from one prisoner to another. Solitary confinement, it was argued, would also prevent idle chatter amongst prisoners and force them to think and contemplate their situation and lifestyle. Only through self-condemnation could true moral reform be achieved. Reformers also lobbied for the improvement of health provision within prisons through better infirmaries, hygiene and ventilation. At Lancaster Castle, the results of this pressure can be seen in the Old Cells, with every cell provided with a ventilation grill above the door and the provision of a window in the Day Room to help circulate air. The idea was to drive out the 'bad air' which was believed at the time to be the principal cause of disease.

The most famous advocate for prison reform at this time was John Howard (1726–90), who visited Lancaster Castle on five occasions between 1774 and 1782. Howard was the son of a prosperous

The Old Cells. Photograph by Carnegie Publishing. Used by kind permission of Lancashire County Council Museum Service

businessman and a fervent Methodist. He was also a wealthy landowner and came from Bedfordshire, where he had served as high sheriff, and one of the duties of this annual office was to conduct an inspection of the county gaol. Many high sheriffs delegated this duty to others, for fear of meeting the prisoners and contracting gaol fever. Howard did not and was appalled by the conditions, noise, filth and lack of discipline that he encountered. This led to a desire to visit other prisons to see if they were any different – invariably they were not, and he devoted the rest of his life to travelling the length and breadth of the country inspecting gaols and writing reports on their conditions, which he then sent to the government. Such was the effect of his work, and that of other reformers working at the time, that parliament passed two Prison Acts in 1774. These included provisions for the payment of salaries to gaolers, the abolition of fees and the appointment of prison surgeons. In 1777 Howard published *The State of the Prisons in England and Wales*, a book which lay bare the deficiencies still inherent in the prison system at the time. For example, with regard to the inmates' diet, he criticised the prisons for the 'want of food' to be found there, and argued that:

> Those who drink only water, and have no nutritious liquor, ought to have at least a pound and a half of bread every day. The bread should be one day old, and then honestly weighed to them... Besides that quantity of bread, each prisoner should have a penny a day in money for cheese, butter, potatoes, peas, or turnips, or he should have a pennyworth of one of those articles.

He also advocated the provision of a Sunday lunch as an incentive towards good behaviour, stating that: 'the turbulent and refractory should not have it.' His work had a profound effect on both the public and parliament.

In 1779 another Act was passed requiring prisons to instigate a regime of hard labour and single celling at night and, in 1784, a further Act provided for the segregation of men and women, along with separation according to crime and regular prison inspections by Justices of the Peace. Justices were also empowered to apply for private Acts of Parliament to raise the required funds to rebuild their local county gaol so that they could conform to the new requirements. At Lancaster Castle, a new set of prison rules was drawn up in 1785, which included a ban on gambling and the imposition of punishments such as solitary confinement, manacling and the withholding of food allowance for bad behaviour. Although not entirely successful, this was an early attempt to instil a new system of discipline and order – precisely what John Howard and others had been arguing was necessary. In addition, the authorities now ordered that prisoners should be clothed in a new prison uniform. This served a number of purposes: it rendered them immediately distinguishable from visitors to the prison; it marked them out psychologically as prisoners (a uniform of shame); and it improved personal hygiene by providing the prisoner with fresh clean clothing. The new rules also stated that neither the governor nor his family was to have any financial interest in the provisioning of the prison. Five years later, the Lancaster justices also ordered that all prisoners be made to work, with refusal resulting in punishment. As an incentive, and in order to provide them with some money on their release, prisoners were allowed to keep a proportion of their earnings. Howard and the other reformers of the period also argued for the provision of chapels and infirmaries to heal the inmates of their spiritual, as well as physical, ailments.

Such was Howard's fame by the late eighteenth century that he was invited to inspect prisons in many countries in continental Europe, and it was during one such visit to the Ukraine that he contracted gaol fever and died on 20 January 1790. The Howard

LANCASTER CASTLE IN 1785

The following extracts from 'Orders and Regulations to be Observed by the CROWN PRISONERS, and enforced by the Keeper of His Majesty's Gaol, THE CASTLE OF LANCASTER' are of interest.

I. NO abuse, ill treatment, quarrelling, or affray to be suffered amongst the prisoners; nor drunkenness, cursing, swearing, obscene or indecent language, nor gaming by cards, dice, or any other method whatsoever, ON PAIN of being punished by closer confinement, fettering and withholding their allowance; which punishments THE KEEPER is hereby required to inflict for the above offences, or other acts of disobedience to these rules and orders; but not to continue any of the above punishments longer than SEVEN days, without making a report of the prisoner's conduct to one or more justice or justices of the peace for the county of Lancaster, and receiving instructions thereon.

II. THE keeper of the gaol shall provide and keep one or more books, in which he shall write down the names of every prisoner who shall behave ill, be refractory or disobedient, specifying his offence and the nature and term of his punishment; and he shall also insert the names of such prisoners who observe these rules, regularly attend public worship, and behave in a peaceably and orderly manner, and he shall produce these books to the visiting magistrates at the assizes and quarter sessions.

III. THE keeper of the gaol, shall not on any account, or pretence whatsoever, demand or take from a prisoner in his custody, or any other person, any money or other matter for fees, garnish money, chamber rents, etc. or for and at the entrance or discharge of any prisoner; and he shall most strictly forbid and prohibit the demanding of any fees, garnish, etc., or other money by the prisoners from one another on any account or pretence whatsoever.

IV. THE keeper of the gaol shall not be concerned or interested, directly or indirectly, in any profits or advantages, to be derived from providing meat, drink, clothes, or other things for any prisoner or prisoners.

V. THE keeper of the gaol shall provide coals, soap, blankets, coverlets, mattresses, mops, brushes, pails, washing bowls, baskets and coal boxes for the NECESSARY use of the prisoners, so that their persons and all parts of the prison may be preserved, as much as is possible, in a state of cleanliness and health; and he shall keep and provide in exact order, scales, weights and liquor measures, legally stamped, for the free use of the prisoners. An account of the same and the expenses incurred shall be delivered in at each court of quarter sessions, who are hereby empowered to examine and allow the same, and to order the county treasurer to pay the amount thereof.

VI. EVERY person committed for FELONY, and every convicted FELON, on being brought to the gaol, shall have all his clothes taken off and be cleaned, washed and clothed in prison uniform; his own clothes to be cleaned, ticketed, and laid up for the prisoner to put on again on his trial or her trial or discharge.

VII. THE keeper of the gaol shall take especial care that every day room, night room and cells be swept clean by one or more prisoners in rotation, every day before breakfast, and washed every Tuesday, Thursday, and Saturday, and he is required to visit every part of the prison, except prevented by sickness or necessary absence; and also attend divine service whenever the Chaplain shall officiate.

VIII. THE keeper of the gaol shall keep a register, in which he shall write the following particulars of each prisoner committed to his charge; viz. name, age, stature, complexion, colour of hair, and place of abode, by whom committed, for what offence, when and how discharged, remarks on the conduct of the prisoner, etc. to be returned at each assize and quarter sessions.

IX. THE criminals in rotation, shall every day pump up a full supply of water for the USE of the prison, and carry the same to such parts of the prison as the keeper shall direct.

X. WIVES and children of the prisoners are not permitted to sleep in the gaol, nor lodgers of any kind.

XI. NO pigs, fowls or dogs must be kept within the prison walls, except the keeper's dog for his security.

XII. THE turnkey shall ring the bell at the opening and locking up of the prisoners in their wards or cells, which shall be opened at eight o'clock in the morning, and locked at dusk in the evening, from the TWENTY FIRST day of September, to the TWENTY FIRST day of March; and during the summer months, at SIX o'clock in the morning, and SEVEN o'clock in the evening. The Bridewell prisoners to be locked in their day wards, during the winter months, from dusk in the evening, until EIGHT o'clock, when they are to be locked up in their cells.

XIII. EVERY felon and Bridewell prisoner shall have a daily allowance of ONE pound of good and wholesome bread, ONE DAY OLD, and weighed out by the prison scales, and TWO pounds and a HALF of oatmeal, and TEN pounds of potatoes weekly.

These allowances of provisions to be given out to the prisoners, as soon as the rooms shall be made clean, but to be entirely withheld from all such as shall not have their hands and faces clean washed, and their persons clean and neat.

XIV. AS an encouragement to industry, cleanliness and good order, and a due attendance on religious worship, an extra allowance shall be made, on every Sunday, of HALF a pound of coarse beef, and one quart of broth (prepared with onions, turnips, etc., in which the same has been boiled) to every prisoner who shall have behaved well during the week - but all allowances and indulgencies to be kept back from such prisoners who have misbehaved and are irregular in attending divine service.

XV. THAT no wine, ale, strong beer or porter, shall be admitted into the Bridewells, transports and felons wards, on any pretence whatsoever unless ordered by the surgeon.

XVI. NO prisoner shall spit on, or otherwise disfigure the walls of the cells or day rooms, destroy or waste their bedding or materials given to them to manufacture, under pain of being severely punished, according to No. 1. 3 days confinement and 48 hours fettering.

XVII. THE keeper of the gaol shall take especial care that the male and female transports, and all persons committed to hard labour, or solitary confinement, be kept in constant work, suitable to their ability and bodily strength. That every prisoner sentenced to hard labour, and every transport shall be entitled to one-third part of his earnings, to be paid when discharged, or removed, provided he hath conducted himself in an orderly manner whilst in prison. And every prisoner in the Bridewell wards, shall be entitled to one-third of his earnings to be paid when discharged from prison, or in such manner and at such times as a visiting magistrates shall direct. Whenever the transports and convicted felons shall refuse to work, they shall not be entitled to the county allowance mentioned in Article 13.

XVIII. THAT the keeper of the gaol shall pay strict attention to the conduct of the CROWN prisoners, whenever admitted into the Debtors yard, for the purpose of pumping or carrying water, etc. so as to prevent any intercourse between them.

XIX. THE Chaplain shall read prayers and preach a sermon on every Sunday morning, and read prayers in the afternoon, and also read prayers every Wednesday and Friday at a stated hour in the forenoon. And that the Chaplain is empowered to purchase at the expense of the county, bibles and common prayer books for the religious instruction of the poor prisoners, at his discretion.

XX. THE Surgeon shall personally visit the prisoners, when required, and once a week or oftener at other times.

The Sheriff of this county and his deputy, the justices at the quarter sessions the grand jury at the assizes, and the visiting and other magistrates are requested to inspect this gaol as frequently as possible, and to enquire how the above regulations are observed by the keeper of the gaol, and his servants, and also by all the prisoners.

THESE rules, orders, and regulations shall be printed and fixed up in each ward.

Lancaster 14th July, 1785.

The 1785 prison rules. Reproduced by kind permission of Lancashire County Council Museum Service

League for Penal Reform, which was founded in 1866, bears his name and carries on his important work.

During his inspections of Lancaster Castle, Howard mentioned that the yard was spacious and that the debtors on the Masters' side had many apartments, including one known as the Oven which had a diameter of 24 feet. This proves that during his visit Hadrian's Tower was being used to accommodate debtors. There was also a Free Ward for debtors which he described as being large but dark in which the inmates could walk and work. Interestingly, he also mentioned that debtors were spinning and knitting in the Crown Hall (presumably when it was not being used for the Assizes), and the Shire Hall (at that time located in the keep). An inscription over the judge's bench in the Shire Hall read: 'Let judgement run down as waters, and righteousness as a mighty stream'. Howard also mentioned that petty offenders were being sent to the castle because the bridewell in Preston (a prison specifically intended for petty offenders) was too far distant. He noted that large rooms were set aside for them near the gate and he must have approved that they were at least kept apart from the felons.

Regarding the felons, Howard mentioned that men and women had separate day rooms in the yard. Women slept in their day room, while the men had two large vaulted cells. There is no doubt that Howard would not have approved of communal sleeping arrangements, as he believed single celling was an important component of prisoner reform. Health was also an issue – he describes one of the cells as a low dungeon, ten steps underground and 21 feet by 9 feet. The atmosphere was 'extremely close, dark, and unwholesome, so very hot even in winter, that coming from it in the morning into the cold air must be pernicious'. The other cell he called the high dungeon; although it was above ground and longer in length than the lower cell, he said it was 'close and offensive'. Howard also criticised the gaol for its lack of an infirmary, but he did acknowledge that a surgeon was provided to treat the prisoners when required. He noted that one of the rooms for debtors was called the Quaker Room, named after the vast numbers of religious dissenters previously incarcerated there.

One recommendation which Howard made was that the stable block underneath the Crown Hall should be converted into a range of single cells. This was taken up and, by 1784, the area had been provided with a row of six prison cells – these are now known as the Old Cells. Each was provided with a bed which ran across the back of the cell and an air vent to facilitate the circulation of air. They are only big enough for one person, although the evidence suggests that more were sometimes imprisoned in them as there are hooks in the wall between which a hammock could be strung to provide additional sleeping arrangements. Outside the cells there is a day room, with a fireplace, in which the prisoners would have been able

Interior of one of the Old Cells; the bed went across the back wall, and right, the solid door with the ventilation grill above. Photographs by Colin Penny. Used by kind permission of Lancashire County Council Museum Service

to eat or socialise before being locked up. Sanitation remained a problem, however, as the only toilet available would have been a bucket. We know that these cells had a variety of uses over the years, including being used to accommodate prisoners awaiting their trial, debtors and, in the early twentieth century, prisoners subjected to solitary confinement for misbehaving. Interestingly, although these cells are undoubtedly Georgian in date, when the door timbers were analysed using dendrochronology it was discovered that the trees the timber came from were cut down in the Tudor period.

The Old Cells, showing the day room with the fireplace in the background. Photograph by Carnegie Publishing. Used by kind permission of Lancashire County Council Museum Service

An old timber prison door with wood dating from the Tudor period. Photograph by Colin Penny. Used by kind permission of Lancashire County Council Museum Service

This suggests that the timber, a valuable commodity, was re-used either from elsewhere in the castle or from another site entirely.

The outcome of this drive towards reform at Lancaster Castle was a decision at the 1783 Quarter Sessions to construct a new gaoler's house, Debtors' Wing and separate rooms and yards for male and female felons. Action was not immediate and an Act to rebuild the prison was not passed until 1788, but Thomas Harrison was subsequently appointed as architect following a competition to oversee the almost-complete rebuilding of a significant proportion of the prison. At the same time, Harrison was also commissioned to construct two new courtrooms, for civil and criminal cases respectively. Previously, civil cases had been heard in a courtroom situated in the keep, whilst criminal cases had been heard in the Crown Hall (now the Library and Barristers' Robing Room). Harrison's first contract ran from 1788 until 1791, and a second ran from 1792 until 1795. He continued to work until 1799 when work was suspended due to lack of funds. Harrison was also working in Chester which meant he could not devote the time to Lancaster that his employers desired. The result was a breach, and Harrison walked off the job. Nevertheless, Harrison had achieved a great deal. The first phase of building (completed 1788) resulted in the construction of new accommodation for the gaoler and his family (The Governor's House), which was built on the site of a pond used to water cattle belonging to the previous military garrison. The archway entrance into this building from the outside was added in 1876. At this time the governor's office was situated in the gatehouse, as were rooms for the turnkeys. The Female Felons' Tower was added in 1793, followed by the new debtors' prison between 1794 and 1796; the Male Felons' Towers were also added in 1796. A wall was then constructed between the male prison and the female and debtors' prisons so that the inmates would not be able to see or interact with one another. The Crown Court and Shire Hall were also constructed at this time, in 1795 and 1798 respectively. Both were constructed in what was, at the time, a very avant-garde neo-Gothic style, with

The Governor's House. Photograph by Colin Penny. Used by kind permission of the Duchy of Lancaster

The Female Felons' Tower, added in 1793. Photograph by Colin Penny. Used by kind permission of the Duchy of Lancaster

furnishings supplied by Gillows of Lancaster. At the same time as this work, Harrison also re-clad the outside of Hadrian's Tower so that the original stonework did not clash with his new structures. Originally, he had wanted to demolish the tower altogether, but the authorities would not allow it. Hence, today it is no longer possible to see through the arrow slits, and from the outside one would not suspect that there is a medieval tower within.

Following Harrison's resignation, building recommenced in 1802 under the architect Joseph Gandy, who completed the interior decoration of the Shire Hall, and, in 1812, added another floor to the Female Felons' Tower. He also constructed the King's Evidence Tower to house witnesses who had 'turned King's evidence'. This was constructed on the site of the former lunatics' yard, and it is possible that lunatics continued to be kept on the upper floors. He also built a set of workshops opposite the east wall of the keep prior to 1807. Gandy's most impressive structure, though,

The King's Evidence Tower, added *c.*1809, and right, the Male Felons' Towers, added in 1796. Photographs by Colin Penny. Used by kind permission of the Duchy of Lancaster

The Female Penitentiary, completed by Gandy in 1821, built along the lines of Bentham's Panopticon Photograph by Colin Penny. Used by kind permission of the Duchy of Lancaster

was the Female Penitentiary, which he completed in 1821, and which was built along the lines of the Panopticon advocated by Jeremy Bentham. This required the complete demolition of the medieval Dungeon Tower which was undertaken in 1818. The Female Penitentiary held inmates on five floors, with an office on the ground floor for the matron and accommodation for an inspector on the first floor. The basement served as a storeroom. In total the enormous sum of £68,860 was spent on improving the prison between 1799 and 1830.

The Panopticon: this was the brainchild of Jeremy Bentham (1748–1832) and was a model of prison design intended to allow the maximum level of surveillance possible by a relatively small number of turnkeys. Essentially, it involved the provision of a tower around which the prison yards would radiate, like a fan, with each yard being triangular in shape. Each floor of the tower would have windows on each side, so all the turnkeys would have to do was turn around to keep all the prisoners under surveillance. It was even suggested that it would not be necessary to have turnkeys in

The Roundhouse (centre) allowed for surveillance of the prison yards. Photograph by Colin Penny. Used by kind permission of the Duchy of Lancaster

the tower all of the time. Glass is quite reflective and, unless the turnkeys were backlit, then the prisoners would not necessarily know if they were being watched or not. Bentham believed that the mere presence of the tower would work psychologically and convince the prisoners that they were being watched. As a result, they would regulate their own behaviour and effectively 'watch themselves'.

Lancaster Castle was an attempt to apply the Panopticon theory. Initially, in 1796, Thomas Harrison constructed the central observation tower (Roundhouse) which allowed for the surveillance of the prison yards. From here the turnkeys could observe four triangular yards. Later, Joseph Gandy added the Female Penitentiary. Standing five stories high, the penitentiary is semi-circular in shape and the nine cells on each floor are triangular (leading some inmates to describe them as 'coffins'). The cell doors were originally not solid, but bars, which meant that a single turnkey could see into each of the cells without having to move very far. This allowed for constant surveillance. Perhaps, not surprisingly, the result of this system, of feeling like they were constantly being watched, as well as the enforced silence, was to drive some prisoners out of their minds. Although a few prisons were partially

Inside the Female Penitentiary. Photograph by Graham Kemp. Used by kind permission of the Duchy of Lancaster

designed along these lines, no true Panopticon prisons were ever built in the UK. The effects on prisoner sanity, together with the fact that the idea proved too expensive to realise, led to the system being dropped within a short space of time. Following the completion of the Female Penitentiary, the older Female Felon's Tower was used to accommodate female debtors.

Elizabeth Fry (1780–1845) had very similar ideas to John Howard regarding the necessity to reform prisoner morals and behaviour, and like him, she saw religion and work as the principle means of achieving this. She did not agree, however, with his notion of single celling and was completely opposed to punishment in prisons, which she saw as serving only to harden the prisoner's character. Born in Norfolk into a wealthy Quaker banking family, Elizabeth married Joseph Fry in 1800 and moved to London. She became very concerned about the conditions in English prisons, in particular the plight of female prisoners and their children who were kept with them. She helped set up a school in Newgate prison and she encouraged women to work at sewing and knitting to earn money so that they had funds and skills to support themselves on their release. Although much of her work was concerned with London prisons, especially Newgate, like John Howard she devoted a great deal of her life to touring the country and visited many other prisons. Elizabeth wrote widely on the subject and was the first woman to give evidence before a Parliamentary Committee. She and her husband came to Lancaster Castle and she was very impressed by the intense building activity and the facilities and order that she encountered. This was just at the point when work was beginning on the construction of the Female Penitentiary – the foundation stone having been laid on 31 July 1818. A local newspaper recorded

Sculpture of Elizabeth Fry.
Sculptor – Alan Ward.
Photograph by Cameron Baird

their thoughts about the prison: they expressed much satisfaction on its plan and cleanliness, order and industry on the men's side of the prison, observing that they had seen nothing like it in other places, and expressed their hopes that the women could be equally well employed and regulated when the new buildings were ready for their reception.

Unfortunately, the official prison inspections revealed a different story at times and the running of the prison by the governor, John Higgin Jr, was even the subject of a Royal Commission in 1812. Higgin had succeeded his father as governor in 1783 at a time when it was common for such positions to be passed from father to son – in 1812 Higgin's assistant was his son, Thomas, and another son, Robert, worked as an assistant to the prison surgeon. The complaint that led to the investigation had been detailed in a letter sent to the Home Secretary by a debtor named Jacob Wilson Wardell, and it contained allegations of serious abuses and misconduct by Higgin and his staff. Higgin was subsequently cleared of almost all the allegations, but the report does offer an interesting glimpse of conditions in the prison at the time of the inquiry. The Male Felons' Prison, for example, consisted of two towers, each of which was divided vertically into two halves to allow for the division of the prisoners into four separate classes, with each class having an adjacent exercise yard. There were eight cells on each of the towers' upper floors, with dayrooms on the ground floors. The yards were supervised from the Turnkeys' Tower.

The keep contained two large rooms; one called the Hanway, which was used for short-term prisoners, and another, known as the Howard Room, for those who had committed misdemeanours. Above the Hanway was a workshop used for weaving. There is also reference to a 'New Tower', which is likely to have been Gandy's King's Evidence Tower. This is described as having a kitchen and storeroom on the ground floor for crown prisoners, along with spacious day room, fireplace, w.c. and water pump. Above there were ten 'airy and well-ventilated cells', which were being used for lunatics and prisoners who had turned King's evidence. There were 174 crown prisoners and 166 debtors, and one of the report's criticisms was that there was too much association between prisoners and turnkeys. Some prisoners were being employed unofficially to help the turnkeys – although frowned upon, this was not uncommon. Most prisons at the time were run with too few staff and trusted prisoners were often used to help with menial tasks. More unusually, prisoners had even served as jurors during an inquiry into the death of a lunatic inmate named Thomas Rawlinson. Rawlinson had died in his cell on 5 May 1812 after being whipped by one of the turnkeys on the 2nd and then manacled for three days. During this time he had broken one pair of manacles and had to be restrained at the hands and legs. He was heard to be shouting at 3am on the 5th, but found dead in his cell five hours later with shreds of his clothing twisted around his neck. Higgin had the body moved to the King's Evidence Tower, and the coroner was informed. Then followed the 'inquest' in the castle, at which Higgin was exonerated of any blame by the prisoner-jurors who returned a verdict of suicide. No notes were taken, and no doctor called. Ultimately, the Royal Commission found no suspicious circumstances in Rawlinson's death; he was described as having a 'furious' temperament, and had tried to hang himself on a previous occasion. Using prisoners to pass judgement on their own gaoler, however, was deemed highly irregular, and Higgin was criticised for having had the body moved. They also criticised him for not keeping proper records.

Ultimately, the debtor's complaint against Higgin backfired spectacularly. The man making the allegations was considered to be a troublemaker, even by most of the other debtors. Of the 166 debtors, 114 had signed a petition disassociating themselves from the complaint, and most gave evidence in favour of John Higgin. The report noted that there was too much freedom allowed to the debtors, too little control, and too few rules. It stated that their apartments were open between 6am and 6pm in the summer and from dawn until 9pm in winter. They also had too much access to alcohol, and the presence of brewing facilities was condemned severely. Conditions within the debtors' prison were also criticised, with poorer inmates sleeping two or three to a bed (albeit an improvement on other reports which mentions three or four to a bed). The Commission report also found fault with conditions in the felons' prison – many prisoners were dirty and wearing rags. Female prisoners were selling their bread allowance to tradesmen supplying the prison, who then sold it in town. Wives of prisoners were even staying overnight with their husbands – overall, prison discipline left much to be desired. Things needed tightening up, and one can imagine how unpopular the debtor who made the complaint must have been with the other prisoners as a result!

Lancaster Castle, like all other British prisons, was inspected regularly by officials sent by the government. In addition, local Justices of the Peace were also required to visit their prisons at least once a year. During these visits they would speak to the prisoners in their cells, inspect the infirmary and the chapel, and peruse the journals produced by the governor, surgeon and chaplain. They would also interview the governor and his staff concerning the running of the prison and leave instructions regarding any improvements necessary. These inspections were crucial if improvements were to continue within the British penal system, but to historians they now offer fascinating insights into how local prisons were operating at the time of the inspections.

In the previous chapter, we noted that Samuel Bamford had complained of being unable to breathe in his cell during his stay in 1819. Prison inspectors often commented that the male felons' towers – though built only 20 years before – were lacking in both light and ventilation. The rest of the castle, with its ancient structures and layout, was completely unsuitable as a prison. They claimed the medieval fabric seriously interfered with arrangements for discipline and convenience. Being damp and cold, the castle also had a negative impact on the health of the prisoners.

The 1812 Commission report described the typical prison day. At first light in winter, or at a fixed hour in summer, the prison bell would ring, and prisoners were allowed ten minutes to dress. Their cell would then be unlocked, and they would be led to the bathroom to wash, and then to work. Next came breakfast followed by attendance at chapel for 30 minutes. Work then took up the period between chapel and lunch, after which they would be led into the castle courtyard for exercise which usually involved walking around the perimeter. Another period of work then followed before supper, which was then followed by either lock up, exercise, or a period of free time prior to lock up.

By 1819, Lancaster Castle held 390 inmates, who were divided into nine classes – 200 males in seven classes, 150 debtors in one class, and 40 females in one class. A year later, this had risen to 420 inmates in 12 classes – the rise being accounted for by an increase in the number of female prisoners to 70. By 1824 the prison had 136 separate cells but could hold up to 495 prisoners. The prison also had 74 workrooms, 32 dayrooms and 12 yards. Overcrowding, however, remained a problem and the prison was still being criticised for this in 1840. In the inspection of that year, Lancaster Castle was regarded as overcrowded and the prisoners were being given too much liberty to smoke and obtain contraband from outside. Convicted prisoners were permitted to write a letter once every three months, unless by special permission, but there were no restrictions on the number of letters they could receive. Those subjected to hard labour were allowed to talk too much and the report included the following damning conclusion:

Aerial view of the nineteenth-century female prison, later the visits centre (right foreground). The roof is a twentieth-century replacement. Photograph by Graham Kemp. Used by kind permission of the Duchy of Lancaster

> The inconvenient arrangement of the interior of Lancaster Castle for the purposes of a prison is undoubtedly a great obstacle to the maintenance of that rigid discipline to which criminals should be subjected.

The inspector went on to claim that the prison had an insufficient number of cells. In conclusion he said:

> No person, however uninformed upon the subject of penal establishments, upon going through this prison can fail of being satisfied but that it is wholly inefficacious for its purposes; that, as to discipline, it is in vain to expect it where unrestricted communication is openly permitted, where prisoners are sleeping three and four in a cell at night, and where the diet is infinitely superior in a great number of cases to what the prisoner enjoys when untainted with crime.

The inspector also noted that Chartists prisoners talked too much about politics and not enough about religion.

On this occasion it seems that the report had an effect, as, in 1846, Lancaster Castle was converted into a women's prison. From that point on, until about 1870, all female felons convicted in the county were sent to Lancaster, and the only men in the prison were either debtors or those awaiting their trial. In about 1860, a new wing for female prisoners was constructed, and a further 20 female cells were added in 1869–70. By 1871, however, the prison was once again housing both male and female felons, and a new Pentonville-style block, known later as A-Wing, was added in about 1871; another 63 cells were added during the mid-1870s, and by 1877 the former debtors' prison was being used to accommodate female prisoners. During the twentieth century, part of the building constructed in 1860 became the visitors' centre and, following the closure of the prison in 2011 and subsequent opening of the site to the public in 2013, the shop and café. The building was demolished in 2017–18.

There can be no doubt that the health of prisoners improved following the legislation and reconstructions of the late eighteenth and early nineteenth centuries. By 1812 there was an infirmary located in the keep, and this tower also housed the chapel and two

Inside A-Wing, added in about 1871. Photograph by Carnegie Publishing. Used by kind permission of the Duchy of Lancaster

sleeping dormitories which held up to 60 prisoners in total. Things were far from perfect, however, as the prison had no drains for sewerage, and the content of the privies was occasionally heaped into the prison yard to be collected in carts and taken away. In 1823 the prison surgeon at Lancaster Castle was James Harrison Stockdale and, in his surgeon's report for that year, he stated that there had been no deaths in the prison, with the greatest number being treated in the hospital at any one time being five. He also mentioned that the prison was healthy, with a good standard of discipline, cleanliness, and ventilation. All told, there were 76 deaths in the prison in the 14 years between 1822 and 1836, with cholera and dysentery accounting for eight fatalities. Gaol fever continued to be a problem in most prisons of the period. The most frequent common ailments were colds, coughs, and stomach complaints.

Malingering was not infrequent, with some prisoners attempting to get out of work by mixing lime from the walls (lime wash was used as a disinfectant to help prevent disease) with soft soap to create a substance which burned ulcers into their legs.

In the 1840 prison report, the surgeon stated that:

> The prisoners enjoy a superior diet to those of their class beyond the walls; at the same time, I think it not a particle more than they ought to have, for the long time they are shut up, and the depressing nature of the confinement.

Reports also show the surgeon visiting all the prisoners at least twice a week. The exceptions were the debtors. Here, he stated, they were hardly ever in their rooms when he called, and he highlighted the free availability of alcohol as having a detrimental effect on their condition. Seven years later, boredom was highlighted as the biggest problem amongst prisoners, but Lancaster Castle was still considered by most inmates to be the best prison in the county. One prisoner commented that the governor was humane, and the prison inspector stated that:

> The prisoners are frequently heard to declare themselves a great deal worse off out of the prison than within.

Education was also promoted within the Victorian prison. At Lancaster Castle there was a library which the prisoners could use, but, as it only contained religious texts, it may be wondered if it was used as frequently as the authorities had hoped it would be. Nevertheless, books were circulated every Saturday. Children would often accompany their mothers into prison if there was no one else to look after them, and, in 1840, there were between 15 to 16 pupils attending the school set up there for their education.

Daily attendance at the chapel for divine worship was compulsory for most convicts, and religion was seen as another means by which prisoners could be taught to embrace a better way of life.

The chaplain played an active role in the life of the prison, and his remit also included working with those involved in healthcare and education within the prison. He also officiated at executions. Provision was also made for Catholic and non-conformist prisoners, who received visits from priests and ministers when required. The longest-serving chaplain at Lancaster Castle was the Reverend Joseph Rowley (1773–1864), who held the office for 54 years. During part of this time (1802–12) Joseph also served as headmaster of the local grammar school.

In 1836, the weekly diet for prisoners sentenced to hard labour was as follows:

> 7lb of wheaten bread
> 2.5lb of oatmeal
> 10lb of potatoes
> 1.5lb of beef
> 5oz of rice
> 1.5 gills of peas
> 4oz cheese

The following meals were served:

> Sunday: one quart of stew made from cow shins in the proportion of one shin to every 14 prisoners.
> Monday: half a pound of boiled beef with potatoes
> Tuesday: one quart of rice soup and potatoes
> Wednesday: half a pound of boiled beef and potatoes
> Thursday: one quart of pea soup and potatoes
> Friday: half a pound of boiled beef made into scouse
> Saturday: Potatoes and cheese.

In 1841 prison clothing consisted of the following:
For males

> Jacket (woollen in winter)
> Waistcoat
> Trousers (x2)
> Woollen cap
> Night caps (x2)
> Underwear

Pocket handkerchief (x2)
Cotton neckerchief (in summer)
Clogs
Shirt
Pair woollen stockings (x2)

The colours were yellow and blue (convicted felons), blue (misdemeanants), and brown (untried).

For females

Woollen petticoat
Under petticoat
Shifts (x2)
Bedgown
Petticoat
Night cap (x2)
Pair woollen stockings (x2)
Pocket handkerchief (x2)
Neckerchiefs (x2)
Apron
Plain caps (x2)
Clogs.

Prisoners' bedding consisted of a hair mattress, two blankets (increased to three in winter) and a rug.

Punishment for breaking the rules at Lancaster Castle consisted of being deprived of Sunday dinners, manacling, or solitary confinement in a dark cell for three days on a diet of bread and water. Other punishments were allowed, but only if authorised by a magistrate – these included the crank, a flogging in the prison yard, or shot drill. The latter involved carrying a 26lb cannonball backwards and forwards across the courtyard, putting it down and picking it up at the end of each leg. It seems that these proved not to be much of a deterrent as prison inspection reports mention that the punishment book displayed a catalogue of insubordination, violence, stealing and refusing to work. Bullying was also an endemic problem, with some prisoners beaten if they were thought to be co-operating or working too hard. The debtors were also very difficult to control. On 30 August 1820, a number of debtors, who

Punishments included shot drill, where miscreants were required to carry a 26lb cannonball backwards and forwards across the courtyard. Photograph by Colin Penny. Used by kind permission of Lancashire County Council Museum Service

were being kept in the former Tap, broke up some furniture and set fire to it. Fortunately, the fire was quickly extinguished before anyone was hurt or the building was damaged.

A number of different forms of hard labour were used at Lancaster Castle. These included the treadwheel, the first of which was installed in 1821. Another wheel was added later – the first treadwheel-powered machinery – and required 13 prisoners at a time (powering 23 pairs of power looms for weaving calico), whilst the other treadwheel pumped water from a well and required 12 prisoners at a time. Like most other treadwheels, those at Lancaster Castle had wooden partitions along them to prevent prisoners talking to each other. From May to October they would walk the treadwheel for ten hours per day, doing 96 steps per minute and climbing 10,400 feet each day; they were allowed a five-minute rest for every 15 minutes of climbing. Females and prisoners under the age of 14 were exempt from this form of hard labour. Treadwheels were finally abolished by the 1898 Prison Act.

Other prisoners were set to work making and repairing shoes and clothes, winding wool, tailoring, hammock-making or (from 1862) oakum-picking. The latter was a task hated by many prisoners as it was monotonous, painful and labour-intensive. It was also a form of recycling; the worn-out rigging from sailing ships was cut into small pieces (about 2 feet each) and sent to county gaols (and workhouses) throughout the country to be 'picked'. Prisoners spent hours carefully separating all of the individual strands of hemp that comprised the rope by rubbing it on their legs and teasing it apart using a small hook and their fingers. Before they could even begin this process, they also had to pick off a layer of tar which had been applied to the rope in order to protect it from the worst effects of the elements whilst at sea. The rooms in which this work was done were filled with dust; prisoners' legs and fingers would be blistered, and their backs and shoulders would ache due to their spending hours hunched over their work. Once separated out, the hemp would then be sent back to the shipyards to be remixed with tar and used as caulking (waterproofing) on the inside of new vessels. At Lancaster Castle, prisoners were also employed unpicking cotton with each inmate picking about one and a half pounds per day. Any wages owed to them for working were paid on their release.

Another form of monotonous hard labour was the crank and it was extremely unpopular with prisoners. At first sight, the crank looked fairly harmless: it consisted of a pedestal on the top of which was a wooden box with a handle on the side and a counter which registered how many times the handle had been turned. Prisoners would then be set a target to reach by a specified time, for example, so many turns before breakfast, before lunch, etc. The average for an adult prisoner was about 1800 per hour, for a juvenile about 1500. What made the crank particularly unpopular, however, was the fact that the tension of the handle could be set by a prison officer. Hence, a prisoner who had been well-behaved the previous day could have the tension set to its lowest point, allowing the handle to turn rapidly and easily. A prisoner who had misbehaved, however, could very well find themselves having to use both hands, and a considerable amount of effort, simply to turn the handle once. Cranks were usually placed by the wall of a room which had been provided with a small opening so that a prison officer could see the counter from a corridor and keep a check on the progress of the 'work'. These counters could be reset by turning a small screw, and this is the reason why prison officers were sometimes referred to as 'screws'.

By the 1830s, attitudes to prison were changing. Emphasis was beginning to move away from the idea of prison as a place of moral reform towards it being solely a means of punishment. Prisoners were seen as being pampered and prison was not considered a deterrent to crime. Inmates were regarded as better fed than on the outside, supplied with clean warm clothes and shelter during the winter. A new mantra emerged from those writing about prisons at the time – hard labour, hard beds, hard food. The work should not be in any way fulfilling, it should be hard, grinding, and boring toil. The food should look and taste disgusting, and the beds should be hard and uncomfortable. It was argued that prisons should be feared and filled with terror and depression, and that the condition of the criminal should be lower than the poorest law-abiding person. Prisoners were there to be punished and every element of their existence was designed to reflect this. At the same time, the benefits of the silent system, first utilised in Auburn, New York State, from the 1820s, were being propounded. Prisoners were forbidden to communicate with one another in order to prevent the spread of the criminal 'disease'. They would be known by a number, not their name, and only allowed to speak when they were spoken to by prison staff. They would be kept in solitary at night and, when exercising in the prison yard, they would wear a mask so that they could not recognise one another and communicate. By the mid-nineteenth century, prison authorities had become convinced that this was an excellent means by which prisoners could be both punished and saved from themselves. All distractions from the prisoner thinking about their condition should be removed, and the regime should be pure punishment. It was perceived that the problem with the judicial and prison system was that it was all imposed upon the criminal who had transgressed the law. He or she was arrested by the police, they were taken to court, tried in front of a jury, and sentenced by a judge. If imprisoned, they were then handed over to the prison authorities to be punished. Everything about the system was external to the person concerned – it was done to them. The problem was that the prisoner might not agree – inside their head they might continue to believe that they had every right to behave in the way that had led them to this point in their life. Unless they had experienced a change in mind-set, they would in all likelihood simply return to their previous lifestyle upon release. By the mid-nineteenth century this idea had achieved a firm hold.

One way out of this spiral of criminal behaviour was to encourage, or almost force, the prisoner to condemn themselves. Only self-condemnation could convince the authorities that a prisoner had changed and was ready to be released back into society. As a result, by the 1870s, the Silent System was widespread in British prisons, but Lancaster Castle was seen as architecturally unsuitable and too overcrowded to apply it. Nevertheless, during the mid 1860s, the governor, Arthur Hansbrow, the son of James Hansbrow (governor 1833–62), did subject the 'quarrelsome and difficult' to this regime. In reality, it was almost totally impossible for the prison authorities to prevent communication between prisoners. The system was also damaging to the mental health of too many inmates – the idea of intentionally breaking a prisoner's will risked breaking their mind altogether and too many prisoners went insane as a direct result. By the early twentieth century, the Silent System had been almost completely abandoned in British prisons.

Twentieth and Twenty-First Centuries

On the death of Queen Victoria in 1901, Lancaster Castle was still working as a prison and a base for the north Lancashire County Assizes. However, a 1904 prison report showed it to be in a sad way. A-Wing (consisting of 56 active cells) was described as 'rather dark', with the corridor on the ground floor being used as a space for 'sewing the mailbags'. B-Block was the women's prison with 28 cells, and it was noted that women worked in the prison laundry washing all the prisoners' and wardens' clothing and bedding. The laundry was situated in a block next to the King's Evidence Tower and, in 1906, it had to be practically rebuilt because it was in such a poor state of repair. One of the male felons' towers was by now long disused and its cells had been turned into storerooms. Next door was the kitchen and a covered walkway that had been built to bring meals across the courtyard to A-Wing. The former Female Penitentiary was being used as a male prison, with nine cells plus a w.c. on each floor, while the former Female Felons' Tower (next to the gatehouse) was used as the hospital for male felons, as well as a reception area. The Chapel was located on the ground floor of the keep and was said to be in a sad need of paint and attention. The rest of the prison was being used as workshops for the inmates. In addition, the report also noted that cottages outside the castle, numbers 5–19 in St Mary's Parade, were part of the prison's property and used to accommodate married staff.

1914 marked the beginning of the Great War, and HMP Lancaster Castle was closed – this would be the last year in which women prisoners were held at the castle. In 1916 Lancaster Castle became a German Prisoner of War (POW) camp, and locals would watch the POWs being marched out of the gates each day to work on building the new road, known as 'Kingsway' – a road off Skerton Bridge, now used to access Caton Road and the M6. Nothing is known about how the German prisoners passed their time at the castle, but, in 1918 and 1919, there was an outbreak of Spanish Flu which killed three of them.

On 12 April 1919, the *Lancaster Guardian* reported the following:

> German Prisoners' Funeral – The Three German prisoners whose deaths from pneumonia in Lancaster Castle we reported last week, were interred in the Lancaster Cemetery on Friday. viz: Lce. Corpl. Fritz Iwers, Pte Karl Jahnert, and Pte Reinhardt. The coffins were covered with German flags and a wreath was placed on each. They were conveyed in three hearses. Six comrades, each carrying a wreath, accompanied the hearses as bearers, and also three guards. Sympathetic interest was taken in the funeral by a large number of townspeople, many of whom proceeded to the cemetery. On the way the cortege was met by a firing party from the Barracks and the enemy soldiers were interred in the grave receiving a burial with Military Honours, the Rev. T. Mercer, St Anne's, officiating.

In 1962, the three soldiers were exhumed and re-interred at the German War Graves Cemetery at Cannock Chase, Staffordshire.

At 11am on Sunday 11 November 2018, to mark the centenary of the Armistice, the Lancaster Castle Museum Manager, Dr Colin Penny, laid wreaths on each of their graves.

In 1919, with the war over, Lancashire County Council (LCC) approached the Prison Commissioners to see if they could take over the prison, rent free, to turn it into the County Police Academy. The plan was to convert most of A-Wing and the former women's cellblock into accommodation for the cadets, while the ground floor of A-Wing would be their dining room. The keep was to be used for recreation purposes and classrooms and later a police garage was added under the former Debtors' Wing. The Governor's House and the cottages outside would be used for staff and married recruits.

Gravestones of the German POWs who died from Spanish flu whilst in captivity at Lancaster Castle. Photographs by Ann-marie Michel

The academy opened in 1923. In 1929, LCC offered to purchase the entire castle. The assumption was that the Prison Commissioners were the owners, under an 1877 Act of Parliament which had given them jurisdiction over all the prisons in England. A sum of £14,000 was settled upon when suddenly the Duchy of Lancaster declared that it was the true owner of the castle. This led to a dispute which was not resolved until 1930 when the Solicitor to the Treasury found in the Duchy's favour. Following the judgement, the Duchy was not prepared to continue with the sale, but in further discussions in 1931 the Duchy offered the castle to Lancashire County Council on a 60-year lease at £500 per annum. In addition, the Duchy sold the old cottages in St Mary's Parade to the council.

One of the new instructors in the Police Academy was Frederic Hogg. He was an ex-constable of the Lancaster Borough Force,

Frederic Hogg, PT instructor for the County Police Academy. Photograph reproduced by kind permission of Jean Nicholson

but, in 1926, moved to the county force to become the PT instructor for the academy. He subsequently left for a short while but returned as the academy's second and last inspector. His office was below the castle clock and he and his family (including his daughter, five-year-old Jeannie) were housed in the former Governor's House. Jeannie remembers that the house leaked badly and buckets had to be placed everywhere to catch the dripping water. She also recalls the 'top brass' coming to visit the academy, and, when she was asked what it was like to live in a castle, she replied: 'It is very nice, but bloody draughty.' As the cadets were county police cadets, they were not allowed out into Lancaster in uniform. The town was under the jurisdiction of the town police force and the demarcation between police forces was strictly observed. It should be noted that Lancaster Castle has never been part of the town or city of Lancaster – it is Duchy land, surrounded by the city. Therefore, recruits and staff were given neutral blue suits so that they could leave the castle to go into town, or to go for outside training which had to be done in Morecambe. Once in Morecambe, they could put their uniforms back on. Hogg's speciality as an instructor was developing upper body strength for traffic control. There were still very few traffic lights and traffic signals in those days, and he used synchronised India club swinging and later specialised in marching to get the cadets to the peak of physical fitness. He would bring in police bands from all over the country for training at the academy.

In 1932, the flat roof of the former women's prison was causing too many problems, so the block was gutted, given a new roof and converted into the academy's gymnasium with a splendid maple wood floor – woe betide any cadet walking on it in his shoes! The academy had a number of punishments for its cadets for infringing discipline or the academy rules. These included peeling potatoes, using small hooks to pick grass out of the cobbles outside the gatehouse, and polishing the cannonballs of the old cannon in the courtyard. Jeannie remembers the cannonballs were always very well polished. She also remembers that in 1936 the whole castle shook as a Zeppelin-type airship flew overhead. In 1937, the year in which Lancaster became a city, the Police Academy closed and silence fell on Lancaster Castle. That year a speculative proposal was drawn up to convert the prison into a royal residence, ironically for the then Duke and Duchess of York. It was the first ever proposal for a royal residence in the north of England. Plans of the design were drawn up which show that the main palace buildings would have been constructed across the courtyard from the Well Tower to C-Wing, with the latter being used as a library. The former cellblocks would be for the servants. The courts would have remained unaffected. However, the response to the proposal was that it was a ludicrous idea and, as the Duke of York had just become King George VI following his brother's abdication, they would not require it.

With the outbreak of the Second World War (1939–45), the previously empty prison courtyards were filled with the noise of civil defence training, such as ARP gas training. The courts continued to sit and, at the January Assizes, 11 men and 3 women were tried. The youngest were two 18-year-olds who were tried for murder and the oldest was a 63-year-old shoe repairer from Fleetwood who was charged with arson. A man from Ulverston was listed for the intriguing offence of 'carnal knowledge', while another was tried for bigamy. Possibly the saddest case was a young aircraft

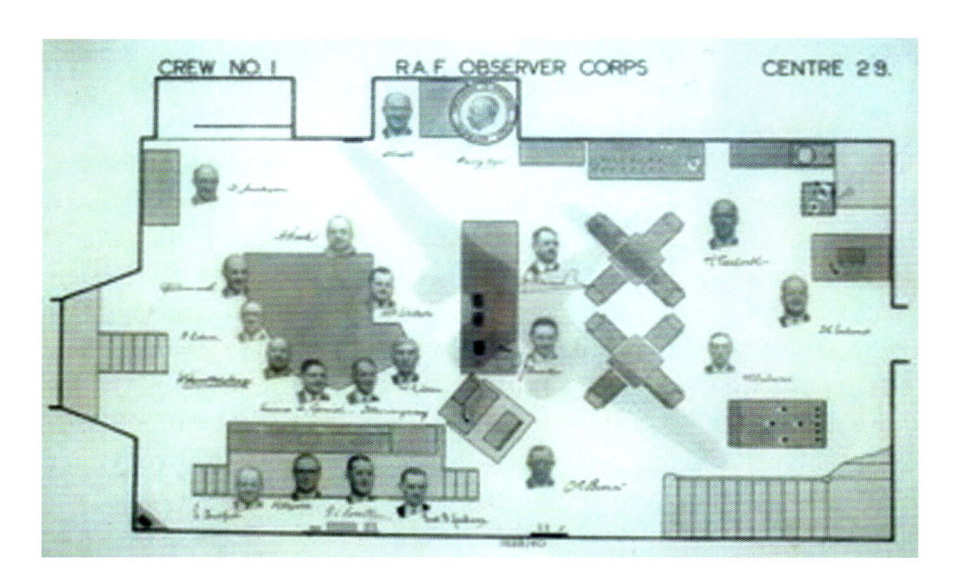

Top: Layout of the Royal Observer Corps 29th Group Operations Room, as drawn by its then members; note the recreational facilities they included for the long nights
Above: The Operations Room in action during the Second World War.
Left: Royal Observer Corps personnel, Lancaster Castle 1946 (L–R) Monica Woods (Typist), Obs. Cdr. L. I. Cowper (Group Commandant), Ronald Brett (Clerical Officer), Obs. Lt. E. B. Morton-Jones (DGC). Images reproduced by kind permission of Tony Hooper and the 29th Group of the Royal Observer Corps

worker and a married woman who were both on trial for conspiracy to induce an abortion.

In 1938, the Lancaster Branch of the Observer Corps (later the Royal Observer Corps after the Battle of Britain) was founded. Shortly after the start of World War II they moved their HQ and operations room into the castle keep, with a subsidiary reserve station under a bank in Church Street. In 1943 the roles were reversed, with the basement of the bank now the main operation room, and the keep as the reserve room. Early in the war a Pioneer Corps company was also stationed at the castle, but in 1943 these were replaced by a company of the Non-Combatant Corps (NCC) who remained at the castle until just after the end of the conflict. The Non-Combatant Corps were comprised mainly of conscientious objectors. These included Plymouth Brethren, Jehovah's Witnesses and Quakers – not the first time the latter had found themselves in Lancaster Prison for their beliefs. At Lancaster, the NCC broke down large shipments of food which arrived at the Quay by rail into individual parcels which were then sent to the soldiers at the front. Also included was the anarchist and playwright George Taylor. He edited an anarchist paper while at Lancaster Castle and one article led to an Old Bailey treason trial in 1945. George and three others were found guilty, but it was all regarded as a rather an over-the-top prosecution and they received very light sentences.

The Nazi leader Rudolph Hess has been claimed as a prisoner at the castle for one night whilst on his way south following his arrest in Scotland in 1941. There is some hearsay surrounding this, but no written evidence has been found to substantiate it.

In 1945, the Royal Observer Corps was disbanded, and the conscientious objectors also left Lancaster Castle. Soon afterwards, however, in 1947, the Cold War began; the Royal Observer Corps was reformed and returned to the castle. George VI and his wife, Queen Elizabeth, made an official visit to the see the Corps at the castle in March 1951.

In 1954, the Prison Commissioners approached the County Council to seek to restore the civilian prison at Lancaster Castle, particularly as by then the Royal Observer Corps was planning to move out. However, a report on the prison showed that it was in a very derelict state. The glass roof of A-Wing had gone, and it was flooded, whilst C-Wing was described as alive with fungi and mould. Much of the castle did not have any electricity, the drains had collapsed, and practically every door, window, and stairwell needed replacing. It would be a mammoth task, and it was estimated that at least £50,000 would be needed to complete the work (approximately £1 million in today's money). However, the Prison Commissioners found a cheaper solution and decided to use the inmates of Preston Prison as the workforce. Work began in 1955 on A-Wing and, once it was habitable, 47 inmates were housed in it as an on-site workforce. In that year, the Queen, in her role as Duke of Lancaster, made the first of her four visits to the castle and inspected the members of Royal Observer Corps at the gatehouse. By 1957, the castle was once more a fully operational category B prison, but the new headquarters for the Royal Observer Corps were not yet ready, so for a while they had to share the castle with the prisoners. Each day, they were escorted in and out and one member remembered the sullen line of prisoners trudging silently around the courtyard. In 1957, the Corps moved out of the castle.

Over the next few decades, prisoners continued to be used to repair and to maintain the castle, and one prisoner made the magnificent weathervane now situated above the Gateway. As the Victorian chapel in the keep was converted into a gymnasium, the prisoners built a new chapel on the second floor, complete with wall murals and stained-glass doors. This became an ecumenical chapel in 1976–77. Interestingly, Lancaster Castle would enjoy the lowest vandalism rate of any UK prison, possibly as the inmates had invested so much of their time into it. The prisoners were kept in three wings – A-Wing, B-Wing and C-Wing. The former police gym became a dining room and then later the prison visitors' centre; this building was demolished in 2018 to reveal the magnificent eighteenth-century cloister which can be seen today. The Well Tower and the King's Evidence Tower were utilised as workshops; the latter being used for training in interior decorating, and many of the cells were beautifully painted and wallpapered. The reception centre was retained in the little tower by the gatehouse and the kitchen remained next to former Male Felons' Tower, which itself

Upper: The former chapel, HMP Lancaster Castle
Lower: The King's Evidence Tower was utilised as a workshop for training in interior decorating.
Photographs by Graham Kemp

continued to be used as the prison storehouse. Later, in the 1990s, B-Wing became a drug rehabilitation block.

The residential court keepers had undertaken tours of the courts since the early nineteenth century and the first castle guidebook was written in 1843. The first recorded school trip was made on 25 June 1934 by a group of children from Greaves School, Lancaster. Between the two World Wars, a professional guide was hired to assist the court keeper; this was Danny Smith who appeared on many of the early Frith postcards of Lancaster Castle. He was later made court keeper himself. Danny was responsible for finding one of the main attractions of the tours – the Old Cells adjacent to

Danny Smith, court keeper of the castle. Photo reproduced by kind permission of William Jefferies

Hadrian's Tower. These cells had been bricked up in early nineteenth century, but he uncovered them in 1931. To be locked up in one has become a highlight of the tours; an experience that few forget.

In 1971, the Assizes were abolished and the courts at Lancaster were downgraded to tertiary divisional courts. At this time the County Council saw the opportunity to develop tourism further at the castle. Eight guides were hired to establish regular tours, but this had to wait until the summer of 1976, following the conclusion of the trial of the Birmingham Six. Led by the court keeper, Jessie Meakin, in the hot summer of that year, a new chapter in the history of the castle was begun, and the first year saw a record 44,000 visitors arrive. The council began to invest further in developing tourism in the castle, with the Shire Hall being made over, and tours becoming an established aspect of the site. Of course, they still had to work around the courts but that was part of the charm in visiting the castle.

With the 60-year lease to the council for the whole castle coming to an end in 1991, many believed that this would lead to the closure of the prison and the whole castle becoming a tourist attraction. Much excitement abounded in the press with words such as the 'Windsor of the North' and a 'Historical Goldmine' quoted from county and city councillors alike. In anticipation of this, the 'Lancaster Castle Project' was set up in that year. It was an exciting project and plans were drawn up to show how the prison could be converted into a county museum, a genealogical centre, Duchy records office, a military museum, and an exhibition and conference centre, plus with space for restaurants and craft shopping arcades, and with the courtyards becoming a centre for theatre, musical entertainment, festivals and historic markets. The tours would also be extended to include the prison. A major archaeological dig would be undertaken by Lancaster University to examine the whole castle area and a plan to 'collect and record all necessary information related to the castle and is environs from all approved sources' would be undertaken. Ultimately, it had to be scaled down as, on that occasion, the Home Office renewed the lease for the prison. HMP Lancaster Castle now became a category C prison and in this role it was highly successful, becoming the second-best prison in the country for preventing men from re-offending with its superb educational and drug rehabilitation programme.

Tourism continued in the Shire Hall side of the building; records were collected and the guides increased their professional knowledge of the castle and its history. A genealogical database was established on the many convicts transported from Lancaster Castle to Australia, making it a major source of Australian family history. Ultimately, Lancaster University did undertake a limited archaeological investigation of the Well Tower. Here they found a bricked-up spiral stairwell to the roof, with a pair of shoes left on each step. By the year 2000, decisions were being made to arrange guided tours on a more established basis, with tours running all year round rather than seasonally. To help develop the castle as a major tourist attraction, its facilities were modernised and it gained a cosmetic make-over with, for example, new exterior lighting. A programme of talks, pamphlets, plays, books and specialised

Damien Warren-Smith in *Hamlet* (2008). Photograph by George Coupe.
Reproduced by kind permission of Demi Paradise Productions

Gemma North as Portia & Richard Hand as Bassanio: *The Merchant of Venice* (2010). Photograph by George Coupe. Reproduced by kind permission of Demi Paradise Productions

The 'Casket Scene' from *The Merchant of Venice* (2010). Photograph by George Coupe. Reproduced by kind permission of Demi Paradise Productions

Left to right: Richard Sails (Brabantio), Adam Jowett (Cassio) and Gabriel Paul, *Othello* (2014). Photograph by George Coupe. Reproduced by kind permission of Demi Paradise Productions

tours were written by the guides and the castle became established as a place of pilgrimage for Quakers, Catholics, and a site of great interest for those fascinated by the history of witchcraft. One guide, Steve Allen, formed a production company to produce promenade-style Shakespearean plays at the castle. These ran from 1999 until 2016 to great success and high critical acclaim. His work helped to bring the beauty and elegance of the courtrooms to an even greater audience.

> When you are so close to a Ghost that you almost say sorry, or the Prince of Denmark brushes past you on the staircase, then this not so much a night at the theatre, but a theatrical event. (Review of *Hamlet*, 2008)

This higher profile for the castle led to it becoming a venue for weddings, book launches, investitures, plays, opera, and much more. In books written about English castles in the 1970s, Lancaster

Castle gained little mention, but, by 2010, it was well on its way to becoming one of Britain's must-see castles, with both domestic and international visitors.

Then, unexpectedly, the Home Office announced the sudden closure of HMP Lancaster Castle in 2011, and, on 31 March 2011, 800 years of penal history came to an end. But this led to yet more exciting possibilities and the development of Lancaster Castle's tourist potential is ongoing. On five occasions in 2012, the Duchy of Lancaster invited the County Council to conduct special guided tours into the courtyard and C-Wing of the former prison. In the following year, the County Council agreed to extend their tours into the former prison on a regular basis. These guided tours remain one of the main highlights for visitors coming to the castle today. And what a castle it is to come to, possessing one of the finest stone keeps in the country and an equally impressive fifteenth-century gatehouse! It was one of the finest debtors' prisons of the nineteenth century. The castle also houses one of the few surviving panopticon cellblocks in the world. The courts are among the oldest in use and its civil courtroom, the Shire Hall, is one of England's finest Georgian buildings. Its history includes Catholic martyrs, Quakers, witches, and over eight centuries of crime and punishment. It is a place of genealogical pilgrimage for Australian and New Zealand family historians and those interested in the history of witchcraft. Above all, in 2022, through its courts, it remains a working castle still carrying out the job it has being doing since the reign of Henry II in the late twelfth century. Long may it continue to do so.

Further Reading

David Shotter, *Romans and Britons in North-West England,* Third Edition, (Centre for North-West Regional Studies: Lancaster, 2004)
David Shotter & Andrew White, *The Romans in Lunesdale* (Centre for North-West Regional Studies: Lancaster, 1995)
David Shotter, *The Roman Frontier in Britain: Hadrian's Wall, The Antonine Wall and Roman Policy in the North* (Carnegie: Preston, 1996)
John Champness, *Lancaster Castle: A Brief History* (Lancashire County Books: Preston, 1993)
John Champness, *Thomas Harrison: Georgian Architect of Chester and Lancaster* (Centre for North-West Regional Studies: Lancaster, 2005)
Jonathan Lumby, *The Lancashire Witch Craze* (Carnegie: Preston, 1995)
Robert Hughes, *The Fatal Shore* (Collins Harvill: London, 1987)
Stephen Bull, *'A General Plague of Madness: The Civil Wars in Lancashire 1640–1660* (Carnegie: Lancaster, 2009)
Emmeline Garnett, *John Marsden's Will: The Hornby Castle Dispute 1780–1840* (The Hambledon Press: London, 1998)
Christine Goodier, *1612: The Lancashire Witch Trials* (Palatine Books: Lancaster, 2011)
Robert Somerville V.S.O., *History of the Duchy of Lancaster* (The Chancellor and Council of the Duchy of Lancaster: London, 1953)
Malcolm Pullen, *The Forty Martyrs of England and Wales 1535–1680* (Athena Press: London, 2008)
James Walsh, *Forty Martyrs of England and Wales* (Catholic Truth Society: London, 1997)
Sophie Thérèse Ambler, *The Song of Simon de Montfort: England's First Revolutionary and the Death of Chivalry* (Picador: London, 2019)
Nathan Amin, *The House of Beaufort: The Bastard Line that Captured the Crown* (Amberley Publishing: Stroud, 2018)
Alison Weir, *Katherine Swynford: The Story of Jon of Gaunt and His Scandalous Duchess* (Random House: London, 2007)
Frank Barlow, *William Rufus* (Methuen: London, 1983)

Richard Oram, *David I: The King Who Made Scotland* (The History Press: Cheltenham, 2008)

Margaret De Lacy, *Prison Reform in Lancashire 1700–1850: A Study of Local Administration* (Manchester University Press: Manchester, 1986)

Norval Morris and David J. Rothman (eds), *The Oxford History of the Prison: The Practice of Punishment in Western Society* (Oxford University Press: Oxford, 1997)

John Howard, F.R.S., *The State of the Prisons in England and Wales, with Preliminary Observations, and an Account of some Foreign Prisons* (1777) (ECCO Print Editions)

Myers, 'An Official Progress Through Lancashire and Cheshire in 1476', *Transactions of the Historic Society for Lancashire and Cheshire* Vol. 116, 1964, pp. 1–29.